Mary Elizabeth McGrath Blake

Poems

Mary Elizabeth McGrath Blake

Poems

ISBN/EAN: 9783744652469

Printed in Europe, USA, Canada, Australia, Japan

Cover: Foto ©Thomas Meinert / pixelio.de

More available books at **www.hansebooks.com**

POEMS

BY

MARY E. BLAKE

(M. E. B.)

"Short swallow-flights of song, that dip
Their wings — and fly away"
TENNYSON

BOSTON
HOUGHTON, MIFFLIN AND COMPANY
NEW YORK: 11 EAST SEVENTEENTH STREET
The Riverside Press, Cambridge
1882

To

MY HUSBAND.

CONTENTS.

iv   *CONTENTS.*   .

IN WAR TIME.

CONTENTS. V

OF CHILDHOOD.

OF AFFLICTION.

SPECIAL OCCASIONS.

POEMS.

THE MASTER'S HAND.

THE scroll was old and gray;
The dust of time had gathered white and
    chill
Above the touches of the worker's skill,
    And hid their charm away.

The many passed it by;
For no sweet curve of dainty face or form,
No gleam of light, or flash of color warm,
    Held back the careless eye.

But when the artist came,
With eye that saw beyond the charm of sense,
He seemed to catch a sense of power intense
    That filled the dusky frame.

And when with jealous care
His hand had cleansed the canvas, line by
line,
Behold ! The fire of perfect art divine,
Had burned its impress there !

Upon the tablet glowed,
Made priceless by the arch of time they
spanned,
The touches of the rare Old Master's hand,
The life his skill bestowed.

.   .   .   .

O God whom we adore !
Give us the watchful sight, to see and trace
Thy living semblance in each human face
However clouded o'er.

Give us the power to find,
However warped and grimed by time and sin,
Thine impress stamped upon the soul within,
Thy signet on the mind.

Not ours the reckless speed
To proudly pass our brother's weakness by,
And turning from his side with careless eye,
To take no further heed ; —

But, studying line by line,
Grant to our hearts deep trust and patient
    skill,
To trace within his soul and spirit still
    Thy Master Hand divine !

ASHES OF ROSES.

A FAIR blue sea, where mirrored lie
    The gold brown rock in sunshine resting,
The changeful glory of the sky,
    The white-winged gull his swift way breast-
        ing, —
A world of light and song and bloom,
    Where earth is glad and heaven rejoices,
And, floating through my quiet room,
    A laughing chime of baby voices.

Half way across the seaward slope
    With tall green grasses bending over,
Two sweet eyes bright with love and hope
    Laugh up at me amid the clover;
With flutter of a little gown
    Whose flying fold the wind upraises,
Her pretty head of golden brown
    My darling lifts amid the daisies.

Part of the shining day she seems,
    But more divine than all its splendor,

Like some fair light that shines in dreams,
  So softly bright, so sweetly tender ;
The glow upon the rounded cheek,
  The lisping voice in broken sweetness,
More life and love and joy bespeak
  Than all the summer's rich completeness.

And yet — alas ! the woful chance
  That comes to dim the moment's pleasure !
The sparkling eye, the speaking glance,
  The heaped-up wealth of June's best treasure,
Do but recall a vanished bliss,
  As Memory's hand the curtain raises, —
Another head as fair as this,
  That lies below the nodding daisies.

TO ONE IN ABSENCE.

WHEN twilight deepens in the darkling skies,
And fair along the azure fields of heaven
The bending stars shine out, like blossoms
given
To gem the garden paths of paradise ;

When the sweet silence of the summer night
Lifts our tired thought to regions of the blest,
To dreams of God and love and quiet rest,
To glimpses full of peace and pure delight, —

Then with all dearest fancies fair and fond,
My heart uplifts thee, O thou more than
friend !
Near or remote, thy presence comes to blend
My best of earth with all my best beyond !

When dawn uplifts the curtains of the East,
And glancing out, the shining eyes of Morn

Look down with rapture on a world new-
born,
Fair as a bride who seeks her marriage feast ;

When the full chimes of life ring out anew ;
And fresh with strength untried, and strong
with prayers,
We lift the burden of our daily cares,
And smile to find the number grown so few, —

Then, with all dearest duties that have birth
In quiet lives that know not blame nor
praise,
Thy memory lives throughout my tranquil
days,
And brings heaven nearer to the paths of
earth !

A LETTER.

"MAKE haste ! make haste, my darling !— the
    long, long year has flown ;
At last, O best and dearest, my heart can
    claim its own !
I bore the weary waiting, but now the end is
    nigh,
Each little moment lingers as if 't would never
    fly.

"Through days of anxious toiling thy face was
    as a charm
To soothe my troubled spirit, to nerve my .
    fainting arm,
Whatever hopes were darkened, whatever
    cares oppressed,
The thought of thee was always like blessed
    dreams of rest.

"The little home we talked of is ready, fresh
    and bright,
I almost see you smiling beside its hearth
    to-night ;

Make haste ! — I thought my spirit could
  mock at adverse fate,
But when love draws so near us 't is bitter
  hard to wait.

" And bring the fond old mother, God bless
  her ! Tell her, dear,
She will not miss the old land when once
  we have her here ;
The graves she left behind her will wring
  her heart awhile,
But soon again we 'll welcome the sunshine
  of her smile.

" Alas ! the knees I knelt at, are cold beneath
  the stone, —
She 'll be to me, please Heaven, as if she
  were my own ;
And peace and rest and comfort shall fill
  her failing years,
With little room for sorrow and little cause
  for tears.

" Then say your good-by, gayly — and if the
  tears should start,
Oh crush them back, my darling, and hide
  them in your heart :

My arms will soon be round you, my lips
    will ease your pain,
And teach the smile to linger around your
    lips again."

.   .   .   .

Swift came the wife and mother across the
    wave-tossed deep,
Alas for fond hearts' yearning! Alas for eyes
    that weep!
They found a swifter message of deeper
    peace had sped,
And the lips that burned to meet them were
    pale and cold and dead !

"THERE'S ROSEMARY — THAT'S FOR REMEMBRANCE?"

Low in the west to crimson turning,
    The sun like a jewel set in gold
Over the breast of the twilight burning,
    Fastens its mantle fold on fold;
The sea like a maiden's face is glowing,
The sweet south wind is merrily blowing,
Still am I sad, for summer is going, —
        Summer is going, — summer is gone!

Never a leaf on the tree is faded,
    Never a blade of the grass is sere,
Gayer and brighter the flowers are shaded,
    Fairer and fairer grows the year;
Only — who knows what my fancy is showing —
Only the roses no longer are growing,
Only I feel that the summer is going, —
        Summer is going, — summer is gone!

Brighter and brighter the skies are shining,
    Deeper and deeper the fresh air thrills,

2

Larger and fuller the vines are twining,
Clearer than ever the distant hills,
The full tides sweep in their ebbing and flow-
ing,
Nothing is lost that is worth the knowing,
Only I feel that summer is going, —
Summer is going, — summer is gone !

What do I mourn ? Who knows ? For surely
Never was world more fair than now ;
From the harvest moon as it rides so purely,
To the red ripe apple upon the bough :
What do I mourn ? Alas ! no knowing ;
Nothing is lost that is worth the showing,
Only I feel that summer is going, —
Summer is going, — summer is gone !

THE TWO GUESTS.

OUTSIDE December's frozen gates
A blithe new-comer stands and waits;

While one, with gray beard on his chin,
Sits robed in pilgrim garb within.

One bright with hope and life's fresh grace,
With youth's glad sunshine on his face;

One grave and sad with sombre air,
Which knows the weight of grief and care.

One sadly waits, till time shall spell
The message of his mute farewell;

The other, friendly heart and hand
Shall hail with welcome through the land.

———

O Parting Guest! Pause yet awhile
And teach thy pallid lips to smile,

For half the New Year's shining grace
Should deck thy form and light thy face;

Within his golden summer hours,
Thy seed will bloom in fruit and flowers,

And half his glow of life will shine
Lit by the soul and strength of thine.

O Coming Guest! Upon thy face
Let tender sadness find a place;

For half the old year's weight of care
Will cloud thy brow and blanch thy hair;

The grief that crushed his broken will
Must cloud thy heaven of gladness still,

And every pang his soul hath known,
Will flash through time to pierce thine own.

———

Fade with thy freight of memories fond
O Year! to seek the land beyond.

Rise from thy newer realm of bliss
O Year! and bring fresh hopes to this!

While we send up from thankful breasts
God speed and love to both our guests.

SINGING AND SIGHING.

When my heart was singing
  All the world sang too,
  Merry laughed the greenwood,
  And the skies were blue;
In and out, round about, through the tasseled
  corn,
Golden bees, on the breeze, flew to chase the
  morn,
    And adown the hill-side,
    Through the rocky glen,
    Every rippling streamlet
    Danced and laughed again, —
    When my heart was singing.

  When my heart was sighing
  All the world was gray,
  Cloud and moaning breezes
  Hid the light away;
Gaunt and bare, through the air, rose the bar-
  ren hill,
Loud and clear, rising near, piped the locust
  shrill,

And the gloom without us
Seemed to find a rest
In the gathering shadows
Hidden in my breast,
When my heart was sighing.

Between song and sighing
Not a day had flown,
Not a change had fallen
Save on me alone;
Shade or light, dark or bright, from my spirit
still
Came the bloom, came the gloom, painting
good or ill;
So through all the seasons,
Every day departs,
Painted with the changes
Of our changing hearts,
Sighing thus, or singing.

EPIPHANY.

WHEN under Judah's midnight skies
  The Virgin mother clasped her child,
And on the Magi's wondering eyes
  Above the hills the day-star smiled,
They rose with glad and swift accord,
  With hearts to praise and gifts to grace,
And came to seek their unknown Lord,
  To meet their Saviour face to face.

We too have seen the day-star rise,
  When, with some message swift to bless,
God's hand hath gemmed our darkened skies,
  And pierced their shroud of loneliness;
When from its calm the soul has risen
  To unknown heights of hope and fear,
And hears the trumpet call of heaven,
  " Arise, and search ! for God is near."

Grant, Lord, that when the message rings
  Across the trancèd silence round,
We rise as rose the Eastern kings,
  And leave all else till Thou art found ·

Nor wait through fear, nor pause for pain,
  Though toil be long and rest be sweet,
Till we too find our Christ again,
  And leave our gifts at Jesus' feet.

ERIN MAVOURNEEN.

SWEET land of my soul! though the shadows
    around thee
  Have hid in their darkness the light of thy
    brow,
Though thy harp-strings lie crushed by the
    chains that have bound thee,
  And the crown of thy glory is lost to us
    now,
Yet fonder the love in our sad hearts up-
    springing,
A vail of new life round thy torn breast fling-
    ing,
Like the ivy's green leaf to the dark ruin
    clinging, —
  Erin Mavourneen arises for thee.

No longer we rest where the summer light
    dallies
  In a flush of wild beauty, with lake, rock,
    and tree,

No longer we kneel by the graves in thy valleys
 Where our forefathers sleep with their God
  and with thee ;
The hearths that were bright in our childhood
 forsaken,
Like seeds that the wind in its wild sport
 hath taken,
Like leaves that the breeze from the forest
 has shaken,
 Erin Mavourneen, we wander from thee.

Yet shrined in our bosoms, through joy and
 through sadness,
 The dream of thy loveliness never departs,
In toil and in danger, in grief and in glad-
 ness,
 Thy memory lives with each pulse of our
  hearts !
There, there, like a star that to light us is
 given,
'T will shine on our path till earth's ties are
 all riven,
And our dying lips breathe their last prayer
 to heaven,
 Erin Mavourneen ! in blessings for thee.

THE ARTIST'S TOUCH.

UNDER the artist's flying hands
The white keys rise, the white keys fall ;
Now sudden sweet, now trumpet loud,
Above the heads in silence bowed,
The brave chords fill the listening hall.

But if the touch be low and soft,
Or if he strike with flame and fire,
. Through all the changes deftly rung,
The soul of music finds a tongue
To lift its message high and higher ;

For major chord and minor note
Not of themselves the tones prolong ;
But as the rent and·broken seals
Through which the master's soul reveals
His radiant thought embalmed in song.

Dear Lord ! Thine instruments are we ;
Under thy hands we wait alone !

And if thy touch bring loss or gain,
And if it lead through joy or pain,
With still small voice, or trumpet tone, —

We may not care to ask or know,
Nor heed if sad or glad it be,
If, in the end, thy thought may roll
Through every chord of heart and soul,
And bear its harmony to Thee.

THE POET'S RIVAL!

ACROSS my lap the baby lies
  The soul-light dawning in his eyes;
I, bending, turn aside to look
  Adown the pages of my book.

With flash of thought and fair conceit,
  The fair lines run on rhythmic feet;
And sparkling fancies gem the brink
  Of this clear well from which I drink.

But sudden, all the poet's skill
  Is dimmed by something sweeter still,
And all his dreamings, high and grand,
  Lie hid beneath a baby's hand.

I stoop to kiss its dimpled grace,
  I turn to read my darling's face,
While falls unheeded to the floor
  The broken spell which binds no more.

O glow of wit! O prayer of saint!
  O brightest picture pen can paint!

O golden rhythmic rise and fall !
My little love is worth you all.

For soaring thought and wingèd word,
That pierce the sky like flight of bird,
May bring the joys of heaven more near,
' But Heaven itself is with me here !

LOVE'S ALMANAC.

HE came: and down through the gathering
 shadows
The stars flashed far with a sudden light;
Sweet perfume stole from the damp, dark
 meadows,
Glory and gladness filled the night.

He went: and over the morning's splendor
A darkness swept to its shining rim;
Earth's throbbing heart-beats glad and tender
Hushed to a silence deep and dim.

Ah dearest love! The ebbing and flowing
Of time and its seasons are naught to me;
Still is it winter when thou art going,
And summer whenever thy face I see.

OCTOBER.

SHE stands upon the silent hills,
  A tender sorrow in her eyes,
As one whose heart at parting thrills
  With summer's sunniest memories;
While, waking from her tearful gloom,
  With cheeks on fire and eyes aflame,
All nature blushes into bloom
  At sound of her beloved name.

The wild woods weave their brightest spells
  To gem the splendor of her hair;
The wild winds swing their sweetest bells
  And die with all their music there;
The banners of her pride unfurled
  Float on the breezes faintly sweet,
And empress of a conquered world,
  She sees its trophies at her feet.

Back to the world she woos the light
  That died as summer's smile expires,

3

And all the fading woods grow bright
With flashes from her altar fires ;
Yet crowned and pale she walks apart,
Lips moving in a mute caress,
And folds above her throbbing heart
The mantle of her loneliness.

As sometime when the bloom has fled,
The light that marked our summer gone,
When spring's best hopes are ripe or dead,
And life's pale winter hurrying on, —
We stand at eventide aside,
Wearing the robes we hoped to win,
And fold our lives in piteous pride,
All fair without, all scarred within !

SPRING.

COME to the woods, O Spring !
Touch the gray silence, smite the winter's gloom,
Till the dim aisles grow bright with sudden
  bloom
And the fair arches ring.

Come ! we have waited long ;
And in the balmy fragrance of thy mouth
Bring us God's message from the sunny South ;
Waken the wild bird's song.

Over the meadows pass,
Flinging the wealth of May buds, faintly sweet,
In shining garlands round the children's feet
Amid the springing grass.

But not to earth alone :
Some things beside have need of quick'ning
  breath,
Some things beside have known the hand of
  death,
And heard the winter's moan.

There are sad hearts, O Spring !
Frozen in bonds of weakness and mistrust,
Moaning for idols shattered in the dust, —
Come, and their sunshine bring.

Pierce through their shrouded night
With hope, joy, love, and all the gifts divine
That rest within that gracious hand of thine,
And win them back to light !

LONGING !

We who walk the common pathway
Of this lower world of ours,
Sometimes live in double seeming,
Plucking thorns and flowers.

Sometimes know a dual being, —
Moments full of passion gleam,
When the hurrying crowd beside us
Fades as in a dream ;

And the slumbering soul within us
Wakes to an unwonted glow,
Thrilling as the springtime blossoms
Under winter's snow.

Though they call us prince or peasant,
Silken robed or hodden gray,
Equal stand we in the presence
Of that inner day.

And we rise in might triumphant,
Burning with a high desire,

As on old heroic altars
    Flamed the sacred fire.

Longing for the crash of battle,
    When amid the weaponed din
Sturdy spirits enter freely
    Glorious meed to win.

Longing for the good beyond us,
    For a glimpse of Him who waits
Throned within the shining city
    And the radiant gates.

Longing! Is it only longing?
    Are the thoughts that come and go
Still to die like summer blossoms
    Under winter's snow?

Are they only idle fancies,
    Falsely fair to rise and shine,
Or, indeed, the blessed gleaming
    Of a spark divine?

Who shall tell us through the silence,
    Though we ask with longing fond, —
Till we pass and find our answers
    Waiting us beyond!

EASTER.

TWICE from Judea's sunset skies
  The shades of darkness crept,
To hide from Mary's weeping eyes
  The place where Jesus slept.
Gathered the gloom of grief and pain
  The sorrowing earth above,
Since Christ on Calvary's Mount was slain
  And Death had conquered Love.

But when the dawning blushed once more
  Across the brow of Night,
What glory all unknown before
  Flashed with its golden light;
What sudden joy, what sweet amaze,
  Made eloquent its breath?
'T was Earth which sang its Maker's praise,
  For Love had conquered Death!

O Power supreme! O Love divine,
  Who stooped from heavenly bliss,
From that sweet world where all was Thine,
  To taste the woe of this!

O God triumphant, who didst break
The chains of sin for me,
Look down and bid my spirit wake
And rise to life with Thee !

HEROES.

WHERE the red path of battle sweeps,
  Where martial feet have trod,
And Death the ripened harvest reaps,
  To offer up to God;
Where steel and smoke and cannon roll
  Awake the startled air,
You test the strength of fire and soul,
  And find your heroes there.

I too, upon my scroll of fame,
  Have set those names apart,
Whose blood was poured to quench the flame
  That fired their country's heart;
Who looked beyond the shades of death,
  Though doubt and fear were nigh,
And gave each pulse of life and breath,
  That Freedom might not die.

But I have other names beside,
  That you perhaps would scout,
For no great triumph broad and wide
  Has rung their praises out:

No passion shock, no battle blaze,
  Has raised them from the dust;
They have but walked life's humble ways,
  And held life's humble trust.

'T is grand to see the spirit rise
  Before some pending fate,
To see the soul in human eyes
  Shine out divinely great ;
To see men strike against the night
  Of earthly wrong and sin,   .
And scorch it with the scathing might
  That speaks the God within ;

Yet when I read the storied past,
  In which such deeds have place,
While the quick blood beats high and fast,
  In triumph for my race,
I can but think how many a life,
  As true, as strong, as brave,
Has conquered in an unknown strife,
  And filled an unknown grave.

The men who fight through want and war,
  Yet heave not sigh nor groan,
Who show the mark of wound and scar
  To God and heaven alone,

Who bear their burdens, calm and strong,
   Through all that life endures, —
These too are Heroes : am I wrong
   To place them high as yours ?

DECEMBER.

CHILL the night wind moans and sighs,
On the sward the stubble dies ;
Slow across the meadows rank
Float the cloud-rifts grim and dank ;
On the hill-side, bare and brown,
Twilight shadows gather down, —
                    'T is December.

Stark and gaunt the naked trees
Wrestle with the wrestling breeze,
While beneath, at every breath,
Dead leaves hold a dance of death ;
But the pine-trees' sighing grace
Greenly decks the barren place,
                    In December.

Chirp of bird nor hum of bee
Breaks across the barren lea ;
Only silence, cold and drear,
Nestles closely far and near,

While in cloak of russet gray,
Nature hides her bloom away
      With December.

Yet we know that, sleeping sound,
Life is waiting underground;
Till beneath his April skies
God shall bid it once more rise,
Warmth and light and beauty rest,
Hushed and calm, upon the breast
      Of December.

So, though sometime winter skies
Hide the summer from our eyes,
Taking from its old time place
Some dear form of love and grace,
We can wait, content to bear
Barren fields and frosted air,
      Through December;

We can wait, till some sweet dawn
Finds the shadows backward drawn,
And beneath its rosy light
May time flushes, warm and bright,
Bring again the bloom that fled
When the earth lay cold and dead
      In December.

ON THE HEIGHTS.

At evening, when the western sky
  Burns crimson with the setting sun,
When night's sweet calm is drawing nigh,
  And day is done, —

While lingering shadows stoop to rest
  Where the dim valley slopes away,
And fold above its silent breast
  Their mantle gray, —

When down from pastures fair and sweet,
  Obedient to the herdsman's cry,
The lowing herds with patient feet
  Go slowly by, —

Still is the mountain top aflame
  With sunset banners all unfurled,
As one who lifts her heart's pure fame
  Above the world.

While far below in wavering mood
  The flickering shadows grope and fall,

It lifts its radiant solitude
  High over all.

———

As sometimes when with indrawn breath
  We see some well-belovèd face
Pass up the shadowy vale of death
  To God's dear grace, —

Through all the mists of soul and sense,
  The eye of faith, with outlook fond,
Can see far off the light intense
  On heights beyond, —

Serene amid the gathering gloom,
  And lit with radiance from above,
Where heaven's eternal glories bloom,
  And God's pure love.

ONE SWALLOW.

THE day was gray and dark and chill;
 Though May had come to meet us,
So closely April lingered still,
 She had no heart to greet us;
When, with a swift and sudden flight,
 Wind-blown o'er hill and hollow,
Two gray wings swept across my sight,
 And lo! the first wild swallow.

"Alas, fair bird! thy little breast,
 That cuts the air so fleetly,
Should still have pressed its Southern nest
 Till June was piping sweetly.
In spite of cheery song and voice,
 Thou brave and blithe new-comer,
I cannot in thy joy rejoice, —
 One swallow makes no summer."

Thus, in my thought I fain would say; —
 Meantime, on swift wing speeding,
Its wild and winning roundelay
 The bird sang on unheeding;

Of odorous fields and drowsy noons,
  Of slow tides landward creeping,
Of woodlands thrilled with jocund tunes,
  Of soft airs hushed and sleeping, —

He sang of waving forest heights
  With strong green boughs upspringing ;
Of faint stars pale with drowsy lights,
  In dusky heavens swinging ;
Of nests high-hung in cottage eaves,
  Of yellow cornfields growing,
And, through the long, slim, fluttering leaves,
  The sleepy winds a-blowing ;

He sang until my soul took heed
  Of warm, soft-falling showers,
Of dells high-piled with tangled leaves,
  And gay with tangled flowers ;
Of life, and love, and hope's bright crew,
  This brave and blithe new-comer, —
And so — and so — at last I knew
  One swallow made the summer !

4

THE SUNSHINE OF THE HEART.

You ask the boon of wealth and power,
  To crown your envied name,
That earth should fling her choicest dower
  Around your path to fame ;
You ask to conquer in the strife, —
  Take then your chosen part ;
I 'd rather fold within my life
  The sunshine of the heart.

I 'd rather know how thus to win
  A balm from every pain,
Thus, even from the shade of sin,
  Some purer strength to gain ;
To live in hope, to trust in right,
  To smile when shadows start,
To walk through darkness as through light
  With sunshine in the heart.

You only claim from outward things
  Their meed of joy to win,
Forgetting that life's deepest springs
  Must always rise within ;

Forgetting that from Time's dim shore
  Earth's treasures all depart,
While I may keep forevermore
  The sunshine of the heart.

This is the magic I would hold,
  My spell to win me love ;
My wand to change all dross to gold,
  My guide to peace above ;
My strength against the blast to bow,
  My shield 'gainst every dart, —
That I may keep, as I do now,
  The sunshine of the heart.

And you — if when you grasp at last
  The prize your deeds would claim,
You long for a discarded past
  And spurn your empty fame —
If you should sigh, with grief opprest,
  To see your dreams depart,
Come, share my love, my peace, my rest, —
  My sunshine of the heart !

MORNING.

FAIR on the eastern hills are the beautiful feet
  of the Morning,
Waking the psàlm of life and the matin hymn
  of labor ;
Touching with heavenly fire the looming mountains of shadow,
Till the hidden landscape flames in a sudden
  blaze of glory :
Calling with earnest voice the breeze that slept
  in the valleys,
Till it beats with a quicker pulse, dashing the
  mist before it.
Over her laughing eyes the veil of the dawn is
  floating,
Hiding the sudden light that else would startle
  and blind us,
Shading her blushing face, till, casting its veiling from her
She shines on our dazzled eyes, the fairest queen
  of the hours.

Hers are the gentle hands that tap at the
  dreamer's window,
Chasing the shapes away that people his land
  of shadows,
While with a voice that falls like the far-off
  ripple of fountains
Heard through the summer trees, thus does she
  sing beside him :
"Wake ! for the darkness flies ; wake ! for the
  world is waiting ;
Life is begun anew with all its promise before
  you ;
Thine are the golden hours that fill the hand
  of the Present.
Wake ere the moments pass, and gathering
  strength from prayer,
Light on the altar of life a lamp that shall
  brighten the future ! "

Hers are the rosy lips that bend by the sick
  man's pillow,
Cooling with lingering breath the flush on the
  heated forehead,
Waking the smile of hope that fled in the dark
  night-watches,
And kissing the restless eyes like touch of a
  swift-winged blessing.

Memory holds the past, and shrouding her face
in darkness,
Sits by its silent doors and waits the coming
of evening,
Then on its golden hinge turning the shadowy
portal
Bears to the waiting heart the wealth of its bu-
ried treasure ;
But clasping her sister's hand, the angel who
guards the future —
Hope, with her shining hair — walks through
the rose-bright hours,
Cleaving the morning air ; then lifting her radiant pinions,
Rises above the clouds, and pierces the blue
beyond them.

Thus when the sunset sleeps on the old man's
silver tresses,
Shading his weary eyes, he turns where Memory waits him,
Holding again the crown he won in the days
departed.
But in the time when youth stands on the
threshold of manhood,
Daring with eagle glance the blaze of its morning sunshine,

Hope on her shining wings pierces the way before him,
Flushing the path with light that soon will be
lost forever,
Pointing to bliss beyond, and urging his swift
feet onward.

TWILIGHT.

Out of the pearly gates and golden portals of
  sunset,
Crushing the amber light in the shade of her
  night-black tresses,
Weaving with subtle hands the mystical web
  of darkness,
Comes through the quiet air the shadowy form
  of Twilight.
Wondrously fair is she as the star that gleams
  on her bosom,
Holding the spangled robe that airily floats
  around her ;
Wondrously fair is she, with eyes that are pure
  as heaven, —
Eyes from whose quiet light the blessing of
  peace descending
Falls on the cares of the day, hushing them
  all to silence.

Out of the pearly gates she leads to their old-
  time places

Feet that are silent now, — forms that have
    passed forever ;
Gently she draws them near, wooes them to
    sit beside us,
Holding our hands once more, speaking from
    soul to spirit.
Back to the white-haired sire she brings the
    days of his childhood,
Laughter and noisy games, and visions of boy·
    ish faces, —
Days when his heart was light, and all his
    hopes and his longings
Hung like pictures of gold on the beautiful
    walls of the future.
Back to the mother's ears it brings the prattle
    of children
(Grown to be women and men) clinging again
    around her,
Fastens the broken links she lost in the quiet
    churchyard,
And shows her the golden chain completed
    and clasped in heaven.

But to the young man's eyes it shows in the
    dawn of promise
The beautiful days to come, the battles that
    lie before him ;

Flushes of love and fire, victories worth the
    winning,
Honor and wealth and fame, the strife and the
    crown of glory.

So does she weave her spells, till on her som-
    bre garments
Crushed and hidden away lie all the roses of
    sunset,
And a quick arrow, shot from the silver quiver
    of moonbeams,
Drops through the dim gray trees to tell us
    the night approaches ;
Then in her shadowy wings folding the gifts
    she brought us, —
Dreams of the beautiful past, hopes of the
    beautiful future, —
Like to a dream herself departs the mystical
    Twilight.

TILL TO-MORROW.

Be kind, dear love, and never say "Good-by!"
  But always, when we're parting, — "Till to
    morrow."
So shall my lips forget to frame a sigh,
  And Hope smile fondly in the face of Sor
    row.

For if, indeed, it be but little space
  Before our parted steps again are meeting,
'T will cheat the hours to haste their lagging
    pace,
  If memory linger still on thought of greet-
    ing.

Or should our feet diverge through weary days
  And dreary nights, the changing seasons
    bringing,
The flinty sharpness of our lonely ways
  Will somewhat smooth, while thus the heart
    is singing.

(And if, — O saddest chance ! — God's pitying
 hands
 Should wide as life and death our paths
  dissever,
What dearer thought could mend the broken
 strands
 Than thus to wait, until we meet — forever !)

So dearest love, be kind, — say not " Good-by,"
 But ever, when we 're parting, — " Till to-
  morrow."
So shall my lips forget to breathe a sigh,
 And Hope smile fondly in the face of Sor-
  row.

AN INVOCATION.

FLOAT with the dawn o'er the roseate waters,
Brightest and best of the year's fairest daugh-
    ters ;
Come where the blooms of the hill-side are
    springing,
Wake the wild birds to a thrill of sweet sing-
    ing ;
    Come with thine eyes full of passionate
        splendor,
    Reading earth's harmonies dreamy and ten-
        der ;
    Come with thy lips full of love to caress us ;
    Breath of the summer, draw nearer to bless
        us !

Speak to the woods, bid their silence be
    broken ;
Speak to the fields, let their lesson be spoken ;
Bid the closed cups of the flowers be riven,
Holding each chalice of dew-drops to heaven ;

Where the chill touch of the winter yet lingers,
Holding life crushed in the clasp of its fingers,
Break the dim shadow of ruin and sadness;
Smile of the summer, wake sunshine and
gladness !

Come to our lives with thy mission of healing;
Wreathe thy fresh bloom o'er the old scars of
feeling ;
Whisper the message God gives to thy keep-
ing, —
Light for the darkness and joy for the weep-
ing ;
Where our souls wait full of darkness and
glooming,
Bid hope arise to make glad with its bloom-
ing ;
Draw back the vail from the grave's shrouded
portal !
Spirit of summer, show life is immortal !

OUR RECORD.

WHO casts a slur on Irish worth, a stain on
Irish fame, —
Who dreads to own his Irish blood or wear
his Irish name, —
Who scorns the warmth of Irish hearts, the
clasp of Irish hands?
Let us but raise the vail to-night and shame
him as he stands.

The Irish fame! It rests enshrined within its
own proud light,
Wherever sword or tongue or pen has fashioned deed of might;
From battle charge of Fontenoy to Grattan's
thunder tone,
It holds its storied past on high, unrivaled
and alone.

The Irish blood! Its crimson tide has watered
hill and plain
Wherever there were wrongs to crush, or free-
men's rights to gain;

No dastard thought, no coward fear, has held
    it tamely by
When there were noble deeds to do, or noble
    deaths to die !

The Irish heart ! The Irish heart ! God keep
    it fair and free,
The fullness of its kindly thought, its wealth
    of honest glee,
Its generous strength, its ardent faith, its un-
    complaining trust,
Though every worshiped idol breaks and crum-
    bles into dust.

And Irish hands, — aye, lift them up ; em-
    browned by honest toil,
The champions of our western world, the
    guardians of the soil ;
When flashed their battle swords aloft, a wait-
    ing world might see
What Irish hands could do and dare to keep
    a nation free.

They bore our starry flag above through bas-
    tion, gate, and wall,
They stood before the foremost rank, the
    bravest of them all ;

And when before the cannon's mouth they
    held the foe at bay,
O never could old Ireland's heart beat prouder
    than that day !

So when a craven fain would hide the birth-
    mark of his race,
Or slightly speak of Erin's sons before her
    children's face,
Breathe no weak word of scorn or shame, but
    crush him where he stands
With Irish worth and Irish fame, as won by
    Irish hands.

5

JUNE.

An odorous breath of drowsy noon
  Creeping across the tangled grass ;
The locust's hum, the cricket's tune,
  The wild birds singing as they pass ;

Mist where the distant mountains rise,
  Mist where the valleys nearer lie,
Veiling the light of nature's eyes,
  Wrapping together earth and sky ;

Tremulous boughs of waving trees
  Raining down shadows cool and fair,
Murmurous sighing summer breeze
  Falling across the trancèd air ;

Mirroring back the azure dome
  Lies the lake by the pine-crowned hill,
Only the swell of its silver foam
  Making the silence deeper still.

Wonderful days of love and life,
  Magical days whose siren kiss

Hushes to rest the inward strife,
  And life alone is perfect bliss.

Beautiful days to sit apart,
  With but one friend to share your throne,
Feeling the pulse of that dear heart
  Beat through the silence with your own ;

Until the twilight pale and gray
  Woke on the shadowy evening's breast,
And breathed above the dying day
  Her evening hymn of peace and rest.

AT THE MOUNTAINS.

WHEN first I saw the mountains fair
  Across the drowsy summer land
Weave shadows through the noontide air,
  Like some strong Fate with mystic hand,
I thought that here the soul might rest
  From longings vague of fancies grown,
And gather from that silent breast
  A deeper calm to fill its own.

But when a few short days had crept
  Across the distance dim and sweet,
The past with all its memories swept
  And left its message at my feet ;
The dreams that lurk in future years,
  The hopes that rise, the fears that pall,
Life's thoughts and wiles, her smiles and tears,
  Came back, and magic tinted all.

For looking from my calm retreat
  All things grew bright as from above ;
The noisy city's dusty street,
  That holds the little home I love ;

The humble path my feet had known,
　The well-known faces round my way,
The little cares, now blessed grown,
　Looked fair as gifts from God to-day.

And so, I mused, — till life's short span
　Is lost beyond the days of time;
New chords will touch the heart of man,
　And seem to ring a sweeter chime;
But when their transient music dies,
　We turn to taste the purer bliss
Of home, and love, and human ties,
　Which make a heaven of worlds like this.

AN AUTUMN THOUGHT.

ABOVE the hills the golden leaflets shine,
  And crimson sunset clouds are brightly
    drifting,
Like gorgeous vailings which a Hand divine
  Between His world and ours is slowly lifting,
    While yellow harvest grain
    Is bright'ning all the plain.

A glory rests upon the silent land,
  More beautiful than summer's fairest bloom-
    ing,
The wondrous cunning of a Master's hand
  That hides away decay and death and gloom-
    ing,
      And gives us Autumn's grace
      Ere Winter comes apace.

The tender dawning of the May-time's bloom,
  The fair June days with all their passing
    sweetness,

Rise up again like shadows from the tomb,
  To find the measure of their full complete-
      ness
        Blazoned on vale and height,
        Beneath October's light.

A mystic peace is brooding in the air,
  A subtle charm the quiet valley folding,
And memory walks beside me, everywhere,
  Like some fair Fate my inmost fancies hold-
      ing,
        To fill with peace divine
        This longing heart of mine.

I sit and muse, not darkly and apart,
  The lesson of its bloom and brightness rob-
      bing,
But where each pulse of mother Nature's heart
  Sets all my blood in joyous measure throb-
      bing,
        Amid the` ripened sheaves
        And glowing Autumn leaves;

And think that thus in solemn splendor dressed,
  As one by one the ties of earth do sever,

The soul of man should seek its winter rest
To find, far off, the Spring which blooms
    forever,
        Where love and hope and truth
        Are bright with heaven's own youth.

WITHOUT AND WITHIN.

WHEN the June roses budded and bloomed,
  Flinging their sensuous fragrance high,
When the June sunsets goldened and gloomed,
  Fading away in the amber sky, —
I stood mid the rustling trees below,
  And these were the words my thought would
    spin, —
"Though green leaves shimmer and fair winds
    blow,
  'T is cold, cold winter, my heart within."

For far away in a stranger's land,
  Where the Southern Cross gleamed high
    ⸱above,
Was the fond, fond heart and the helping hand,
  And the tender eyes of mine own true love;
So mid the passionate breath of the rose,
  And clamor of birds the wild wood in,
I said to myself, in the orchard close,
  "'T is cold, cold winter my heart within."

Now in the dim December night
  The bare trees shiver in icy mail,
And under the spectral moonbeams' light,
  The snow wreaths shine on the frozen vale ; —
Cold is the blast of the north-wind's breath,
  But these are the words my thought would
    spin, —
" The earth lies still in the garb of death,
  But O ! 't is summer my heart within."

There is a heart beats close to mine
  Come to me out of the land beyond ;
There are dear eyes whose glances shine,
  There is a hand clasp close and fond.
Winds may whistle and tempests roar,
  None to my heart can enter in ;
Here in the twilight I sing once more, —
  " 'T is winter without, but summer within."

AT EVENTIDE.

| THE day is done.
Soft as a dream the sunset fades and dies,
And silent stars amid the dusky skies
  Shine one by one.

The shadows wait,
And climbing upward over spire and towers,
Seem drawing softly this dull earth of ours
  To heaven's gate.

We wait the night
With no vain thought of darkness or of dread,
But dreams of peace for weary heart and head,
  And slumbers light;

We wait, nor fear
The few short hours of silence and of gloom,
Before the eastern skies shall blush with bloom,
  And morn be near.

 • • • • • •

My God! my All!
When the dim hour draws near us, by Thy grace

To meet the white death angel face to face,
And hear Thy call, —

When life. lies low, —
A gasping shadow by the altar-stair,
That leadeth up from darkness unaware
To heaven's glow, —

Thus let us wait ;
In faith and trust, with prayer and blessing fond,
Still mindful of the morning light beyond, —
Before the gate.

Not sore distressed, —
But calmly folding life's dull garb away,
Lie down in peace to wait the coming day,
And find our rest !

THE CHRISTIAN MARTYR.

(FROM THE PICTURE OF PAUL DELAROCHE.)

I.

A MIDNIGHT waste of waters dark and chill,
  With one pale star-beam falling there to
    rest,
A white-robed martyr floating calm and still,
  As moves the tide above the silent breast;

A cruel cord that holds the lifeless wrist,
  A floating robe upon the water spread,
A tender cheek that loving lips have kissed,
  And uncoiled hair weighed backward from the
    head;

And a sweet face, so full of heavenly love
  As one whom God had saved from dying
    woe, —
One glory rests the quiet brow above,
  Another crowns the silent heart below.

II.

What saddening tale of human pride or wrong
  Breaks the dim calm that broods above the
    sea ?
What human passions, pitiless and strong,
  Thus grasped the weapons of eternity ?

Or what dark pagan, maddened by the strength
  That marked her faith as born of heaven's
    high throne,
Cast her beyond him by a full arm's length,
  And left her with the wave and night alone ?

I may not say ; — enough for me to know
  Heaven sent its peace to ease her passing
    pain,
Till her rapt soul, uplifted, learned to know
  The waking pulse of joy and life again.

For in the pictured face, though cold and still,
  We read to-day, with hushed and reverent
    breath,
Of weakness strengthened by the Father's will,
  And victory gathered from the strife of death ;

Of the great triumph-smile of spirits riven
From the strong ties of natures frail and fond,
Who, daring all of life for God and heaven,
Float out through darkness to the light be-
yond.

III.

Thus when I raise mine eyes and look above
To the white face that floats the midnight
sea,
A far-off voice of majesty and love
Thus reads my picture's lesson unto me :

O thou of little strength and lesser faith,
When pain or sorrow shake thy wonted calm,
See how, at last, beyond life's passing scathe,
God's crown of glory hides the martyr's palm.

SUNSET.

Flame, O fires of the Sunset, where earth and
  sky have met,
Like the flare of burning beacons on windy
  headlands set !

Blaze on the distant mountains, blaze on the
  nearer hill,
While, wrapped in its purple shadow, the valley
  lies calm and still.

Crown with an aureole golden the trees on the
  sloping height,
Fall on the startling ocean in showers of crimson light.

Flame till the veils are cloven, the curtains rent
  in twain,
Till the gates of the temple of heaven are
  opened to us again, —

Till we see the mystical wonders your shining
    portals hide,
And walk in the streets of the city that stands
    on the farther side, —

Till we find the hopes that vanished like waves
    from the tide-swept sand,
When the feet of the loved and cherished had
    entered the Sunset land, —

Till we see with tearful longing, and hold on
    our hearts once more,
The old familiar faces of those who have gone
    before, —

The old familiar faces, yet bright with a won-
    drous grace,
As of those who had met the Saviour, and knelt
    to Him face to face.

Fade, O fires of the Sunset! Fade on the
    mountain crest,
Scatter the ashes of darkness down from the
    smouldering west;

6

Scatter the ashes of darkness down over grave
  and sod,
And, sitting beneath the shadow, leave us alone
  with God.

THE SPIRIT TURNS TO THEE.

To Thee, my God, to Thee,
The soul that Thou hast wakened from the dust
Rises, with all the might of faith and trust, .
    Whether on land or sea.

To Thee, my God, to Thee,
The deathless essence which Thy hand hath
    given
To image forth on earth Thy face in heaven,
    Will spread its wings and flee !

Though other beacons shine,
Though earthly pleasures woo the passing guest,
One gift alone can make the spirit blest, —
    Thy love, Thy joy divine.

When, at the lightest call,
The joyous chords of life in union blend,
It waits until Thy presence comes to lend
    The sweetest tone of. all.

And when, in grief and pain,
The anchors of its earthly trust are riven,
It looks beyond the pearly gates of heaven
To find its rest again.

For Thee, my God, alone,
The waiting soul with deathless longing burns,
And through the mist of distance fondly turns
To where Thy light is shown.

With Thee its pulses chime,
Like the deep swell of that eternal sea
Which pours the waters of Eternity
Against the shores of Time.

Less than Thyself, no aim
Can guide its wayward groping for the light,
Can quench its longing for the Infinite,
Can win its purest fame, —

For it is all Thine own ;
The image of Thy majesty and love,
The essence of Thine altar fires above,
Which burns for Thee alone, —

And turns to seek Thy feet
Beyond all earthly joy or earthly strife,

Beyond the passing weal or woe of life,
    Through vict'ry or defeat; —

    Beyond the land and sea,
Beyond earth's idols shattered in the dust,
It rises on the wings of hope and trust
    To Thee, my God, to Thee!

MY LOST TREASURE.

I LOST a treasure when the winter skies
  Hung gray and low,
And life grew dim before my weeping eyes,
  I sorrowed so !
Then evermore through storm or cloud or shine,
  With head low bowed,
I sought the treasure which had once been mine
  Amid the crowd.

I could not lift mine eyes above the sod,
  Nor breathe a prayer,
Nor call with faith upon the name of God,
  In my despair ;
And when sweet words of comfort or relief
  Would hold me fast,
I closer wrapped the mourning robes of grief,
  And hurried past ;

Till one sweet day, across my tear-stained face
  A sunbeam stole,
A wingèd messenger of love and grace
  To greet my soul :

I looked, and all the gladsome earth was fair
On hill and plain,
While summer incense on the balmy air
Breathed hope again.

I looked : the fields were garlanded in green,
The woodlands rang
With flower-bells, and in the leafy screen
The wild birds sang ;
Then as mine eyes, now clearer grown and
strong,
Were slow uprisen,
Behold ! the treasure I had lost so long
Was found,— in Heaven !

ZENOBIA.

(HARRIET HOSMER'S STATUE.)

THE passive hands
Held loosely by their golden weight of chain, —
The heavy folds of mantle and of robe
Partaking of her majesty, — the mien
So full of royal dignity and grace, —
Thus, with a cloud upon the perfect face,
A shadowy sorrow veiling all its fire,
A world of passion sleeping on the lips,
And down-dropped eyes that spoke the heart
    within,
Zenobia walked through Rome.

             She does not see
The changing looks of pity or of hate
That fall on her from unfamiliar eyes ;
Nor hear the rumble of the chariot wheels
That bear the haughty conqueror. Away
Beyond the yellow Tiber, and the flow
Of the blue sea that laps the Syrian strand,

Beyond the reach of desert and of plain,
She stands beside the temples of her gods
In fair Palmyra. Round her in the air
The swaying palm-trees nod their tufted plumes,
And eastern blossoms drunk with eastern spice
Fling perfume from their honeyed chalices.

She hears within her palace walls once more
Her children's voices playing in the shade
That filters through the garden walks ; or proud
In all the blazoned pageantry of war,
She leads again from out the city gates
The shining legions of her dauntless hosts,
And hears, like incense rising from their lips,
The shout of. praise that lifts her name to
        heaven.

Her heart is with Palmyra as it stood
In bygone days, her glory and her pride ;
Nor in her fiftful musing does she dream
Of that dark hour, when, silent and alone,
She saw the royal purple of her robe
Grow dim forever with the stain of blood
And dust of desolation.

        .   .   .   .   .   .

O pale mute marble ! Most serenely still,
Yet eloquent with more than voiceful thought,
Thus stand forever ! Holding through all time
The passing record of a passing hour,
Rest with the seal of silence on thy lips,
And speak the lessons of a vanished past.

WHITHER ?

Whither, O shining sails that glide
    All rosy bright with morning's kiss,
Turning the clinging waves aside
    To reach some fairer world than this ?

Whither, O shadowy sails that turn
    Beyond the sunset cold and dim,
To where the stars of evening burn
    Above the far horizon's rim ?

Flushed with the eager dawning light,
    Pale with the evening's mystic pall,
They fade before our longing sight,
    And who shall say what chance may fall.

Some turn unknown of law or fate,
    May hide our farthest ken above, —
The seeming spell of some dark hate,
    Or the all-guiding power of love.

For one the tempest's wrath may wait
  To crush life's hopes so fair, so fond ;
While one may pass through night's dark gate
  To the fair morning lands beyond !

AWAY FROM HOME.

THE sunset falls across the sea
  In flakes of golden light,
While the good ship sails fast and free
  Into the silent night;
But while I watch with dazzled eyes
  The fading smile of day,
My heart is with our eastern skies,
  And loved ones far away.

I hear the rippling of the waves
  Like some sweet thought that thrills
When the cool evening breezes play
  On our New England hills;
While at each murmured word that breaks
  Across the tinkling spray,
Some echoing chord of memory wakes
  For loved ones far away.

And as the moonbeams' silver light
  Falls trembling from above,
To shine across the wooded height
  And bless the home I love,

I know what eyes will meet it there,
What soul and lips will pray
That God may hold in tender care
Their loved one far away.

O life is bright as heaven above
When youth and hope are free ;
O earth is fair and full of love
On land and shore and sea ;
But earth would dim and hope depart
If nearer day by day
I could not lead this longing heart
To loved ones far away.

A CHRISTMAS HYMN.

FATHER of life and love !
While the full echo high and higher swells
From the glad chiming of the Christmas bells,
 Lift we our hearts above.

Up from the weary cares
That spring like weeds around the ways of life,
From thorny paths of passion and of strife,
 We mount the golden stairs, —

The golden stairs of prayer
That pierce the secrets of Thy dwelling-place,
And leave us with Thy presence face to face,
 To pour our soul out there.

Hear us, O Power divine !
Infuse our weakness with Thy steadfast will,
That joy or woe may lead us nearer still
 To join our lives with Thine.

· Grant us one little spark
From the white light that burns before Thy
    throne,
To fire our hearts and make them all Thine
    own,
    Though days be fair or dark.

    So shall the time be blest,
Whether we strike with purpose firm and high,
Or stand with Thy mute workers waiting by
    To gain the promised rest.

    And as the years increase,
Here in the flesh, or in the spirit there,
Our souls shall reap the harvest-tide of prayer,—
    Thy Christmas gift of Peace.

FOR AYE AND AYE.

O JEWELED day, so fairly set
  Within the seasons' golden clasping,
O sapphire seas, that toss and fret
  The yellow sands with eager grasping, —
O warm, sweet air that comes and goes
With musky breath of pink and rose,
When night shall hang her lamps on high
Will you be gone for aye and aye?

Fair earth, in all the happy prime
  Of nodding blooms that deck the meadow,
And tangled boughs that creep and climb
  In dim green aisles of sun and shadow,
Bright wings that flutter as ye pass
In tuneful flight above the grass,
When the swift summer hastens by
Will ye be dimmed for aye and aye?

Deep, murmurous calms that brood and sweep
  As if the earth in tranquil seeming   ·

7

Lay hushed by whispering winds asleep,
  And our wrapt souls were with her dream-
    ing ;
Bright waves that dimple as ye run
Beneath the kisses of the sun,
When wild the storm king's banners fly,
Will ye be lost for aye and aye ?

Nay ! for my longing eyes have flown
  To each fair point of joy and sweetness,
And made the living page my own
  In all its rare and bright completeness :
So come dark veil of sombre night,
Come tempest wrath, and winter blight,
For earth and air and song and sky
Shall live with me for aye and aye.

L'ENVOI.

As some dear friend to other climes departing,
  Holding the hands of one he loveth well,
Looks in his eyes while silent tears are start-
      ing,
  And without words they breathe a mute fare-
      well, —

So ere the Spring across the mountains flying
  Wakes the gray earth from silence and re-
      pose,
Let us draw near the hoary monarch dying,
  And bid good-by to Winter ere he goes.

Think when he came, his royal robes around
      him,
  Grand in his strength and glorious in his
    · might,
Minstrel and bard with song and welcome
      crowned him,   .
  And shall he go without a word to-night?

Then was he strange, — no single grief or
    pleasure
Bound to our lives his presence like a spell;
Now, when he holds our memory's dearest
    treasure,
    Shall we forget to bless and say farewell?

Nay! for though fast the Future's ties may
    bind us,
    Fair with the light her witcheries may cast,
She cannot hide the tender gloom behind us,
    She cannot hush the whispers of the Past.

Yet as we bend to pluck the opening flowers,
    We'll think of one, though faded all more
    dear,
And while we touch glad chords in joyous
    hours,
    Some broken echo sweeter still we hear.

For in life's paths of honor and of duty
    Each day fulfills the promise of the last,
He best may hope to win the future's beauty,
    Who best has kept the treasures of the
    past.

So ere the Spring across the mountains flying
  Wakes the grim earth from silence and re-
    pose,
Let us draw near the hoary monarch dying,
  And say farewell to Winter ere he goes.

WHILE SNOWS ARE FALLING.

THE springtime came, the springtime went,
  With shimmer of cloud and shiny weather;
The golden glory of June was spent,
  On hills and fields we roamed together;
We walked through autumn's purple haze,
  The future's dream of bliss forestalling,
And shuddering thought of winter days
      With snows a-falling.

For earth was all so wondrous fair,
  And heaven smiled down so blue above it,
Each wandering breath of balmy air
  But made us learn anew to love it;
What wonder if with all so bright,
  And wild birds through the woodland calling,
We sighed to think of winter's night
      While snows were falling.

But when at last the world was dressed
  In shining robes of ice-mail gleaming,

And calm white silence lulled to rest
   The pale, mute flowers beneath them dream-
      ing, —
Behold ! We woke to find made true
   The hope our hearts had been forestalling,
And life grew fairer than we knew, —
      While snows were falling.

Ah, well ! the days of youth fly fast,
   Their suns grow dim, their blossoms wither ;
And many a dream that made our past,
   Flies fast and far, we know not whither ;
But when we tread life's wintry slope
   We hear again their voices calling,
And Memory leads us back to Hope
      While snows are falling.

THE DIFFERENCE.

I KNOW that fortune's happier star
  Has marked for you a brighter lot,
Has wrapped your life from wound and scar,
  And bid earth's shadows be forgot, —
    While I, outside the charmèd gate,
    Have learned to struggle, toil, and wait.

I know that to your baby brow
  The golden crown of wealth was given,
The golden wand, whose mandates bow
  More hearts than either God or heaven, —
    While I, in poor but proud content,
    Have coined my fortunes as I went.

I know you boast ancestral earls,
  And scutcheoned shield and blazoned pride,
Thus heralding to earth's poor churls
  How long ago YOUR heroes died, —
    While I, no aid from friend or pelf,
    Begin my record with myself.

Yet what of this? You nobly born,
  I from the people called to rise,
Is this enough to task your scorn,
  Or cause a sneer to blind your eyes?
    Then pause a moment ere you go, —
    I do not read the difference so.

I know you dead to honest faith,
  And useless with your idle hands,
And stunted by the frozen weight
  Of pale, dead honors, house and lands, —
    While I, for share in God's great will,
    Keep heart and hope unsullied still.

I know you lost to honest shames,
  And false where noble souls aspire,
And trammeled close by petty aims,
  A puppet drawn by Fashion's wire, —
    While I, along life's devious way,
    Still clamber upward day by day.

You have a Present, dead and calm,
  No grime to soil your finger-tips,
A perfumed waste of flowers and balm,
  But dead-sea apples to the lips ; —
    I toil and trust with manhood's fire,
    To bring to light my soul's desire.

And then a Future comes. You wait
  Or shudder as the thought comes nigh
Of that dread time, when chance or fate
  Will call your mightiness — to die.
    I, through all pain, within my breast
    Still hold the promised boon of rest.

So though I own you nobly born,
  Above me, by the world's decree,
I answer back your scorn with scorn,
  And smile upon your high degree, —
    Content while heart and soul are given
    For life on earth and faith in heaven.

COMPENSATIONS.

"Why must we mourn for vanished light,
   For pleasures lost, as fair as fleeting,
And weep beneath the eyes of night
   The memory of our morning greeting?
Is joy too weak to live alway?
   Is life so fond of pale-browed sorrow,
That every hope which blooms to-day
   Must fade and die before to-morrow?"

But — "Nay," — a voice within replied,
   So sweet I could not choose but hear it, —
"God never yet hath light denied
   To those whose souls can draw them near it,
Look up in trust, and see beyond
   These clouds of ill, this vain repining,
A Father's strength sustained and fond,
   A Father's love securely shining."

But doubting still and weak, I moan:
   "Your heaven's too far — give something
      nearer;

Why are we left to stand alone,
With all gone by that made life dearer?
The friends we seek clasp hands and part,
    The souls we love draw throbbing near us,
Eye speaks to eye, heart leans on heart,
    Then naught remains to help or cheer us!"

"And yet, and yet,"—the voice rang clear,
    And proud as love and faith could make it,—
"While memory holds your friendship near
    Can loss or change or sorrow break it?
Soul meets with soul;—an instant's ray
Can forge a chain no time can sever;
Through life, through death, by night and day,
Thus meeting once they meet forever!"

IN AUTUMN.

THE golden haze of Autumn creeps and dallies
    Above the far horizon's misty rim ;
The golden lights of Autumn fire the valleys,
    While summer's fading beauties pale and dim.

And mellowed to a pure and deeper measure,
    The murmuring wind sings lullabies of rest,
Low crooning to the safe and garnered treasure
    That lies secure on Nature's loving breast.

Forgot in happier sense of full fruition,
    The grime and heat of labor's unrest cease ;
Earth sleeps from all the dreams that wait am-
    bition,
    And joins with heaven in one fair hymn of
    peace.

On what blest scene of love and joy supernal,
    Beyond Time's changes safe and far away,

Do thy dear eyes, made glad with life eternal,
O child beloved! look out and rest to-day?

What change has crept above thy boyish beauty?
What joys have added sweetness to thy smile?
What unknown bliss of higher hope and duty
    Has crowned the brow we knew and kissed
    erewhile?

And how are they — the well-beloved and cher-
    ished —
Who by thy side have sought the land beyond,
Beside whose graves life's fairest dreams have
    perished, —
    Are they still ours, the darlings fair and fond?

Thy brothers' voices in mine ear are ringing,
    Their footsteps bound above the sun-brown
    sod,
But O for one swift glance, where, gladly spring-
    ing,
    Thy white feet press the happy fields of God!

O for one instant wild with bliss immortal,
    And mad with fullness of delight and pain, —

To enter in at heaven's unguarded portal,
  And catch the love-light of thine eyes again!

Sometime! sometime! O God, that dealeth
    kindly,
  The day must come when grief and tears shall
    cease,
And life's torn hearts, that weep and smile so
    blindly,
  Rest in the autumn sweetness of Thy peace.

VALE.

HAIL, and farewell! O balm and bane
  Of earthly joy and earthly sorrow!
We only meet to part again,
  And night still shrouds the brightest morrow.

One day, and drunken with delight,
  The wild bird sings to each new-comer;
The next, he wings his alien flight,
  To find far off the vanished summer.

One moment, and our hearts have flown
  Through clasping hands and fond lips meet-
      ing;
The next, we stand and wait alone,
  While memory holds the place of greeting.

O promised land, supremely fair,
  To whose blest height our feet are turning!
Of all thy gifts most strange and rare
  For which our longing hearts are burning, —

Will any be so sweet as this:
  That when the soul, — divinely shaken
By that first throbbing pulse of bliss
  Which bids its slumbering sense awaken, —

Shall turn to meet its God at last,
  In that "All hail!" so sweet and tender?
Farewell shall evermore be cast
  From heaven's eternal light and splendor!

Nor, through all time, shall parting rend,
  Or grief bemoan, or loss dissever,
But fair lost hope and fair lost friend
  Once more our own, be ours forever!

8

MUSTERED OUT.

WHERE the blessèd winter sunshine close beside
    my pallet falls,
While I watch its golden glory steal across the
    white-washed walls,
While I hear amid the silence Christmas chime
    and Christmas shout, —
        I am lying,
        Faint and dying,
    Waiting to be mustered out.

'T is the time, I well remember, when I hoped
    once more to stand
Safe within the charmèd circle of the joyous
    household band,
Grim, perhaps, with warlike scarring; proud, per-
    haps, of warlike fame ; —
        Vain my dreaming, —
        Yet in seeming
    I can think it just the same.

Weeks ago my comrades parted, — the brave
    remnant tried and strong,
Who had stemmed the tide of battle and the
    wreck of war so long;
When I heard the well-known voices tremble
    as they said good-by,
        Doubting, fearing,
        Death still nearing,
    It seemed bitter, hard to die.

For I seemed to hear the greeting, seemed to
    see the welcoming eyes,
Waiting me beside the hearthstone under our
    New England skies, —
Waiting till the brown eyes faded, waiting till
    the cheeks grew white, —
        God, who readeth
        All, and heedeth,
    Knows how dark my thoughts that night.

But 't is past: I thank His mercy that the mists
    have flown away,
And within the purer dawning leading to the
    perfect day,
I can read His hidden meaning through the
    shadows wrapped about,

Own my weakness,
And with meekness
Wait in peace the mustering out.

I can thank Him for the spirit that upheld my
    shrinking soul,
Nerved the arm and pointed onward with a
    power beyond control,
For the strength of fire and manhood, — yea,
    for even wound and groan,
        Partial giving
        Is our living,
    But to die makes all His own.

He will hold the trusts I leave Him; He will
    guard the trembling feet;
He will shield through pain and sorrow, win-
    ter's cold and summer's heat;
And when through the Christmas chiming I
    shall hear my name without,
        Close beside me,
        He will guide me; —
    So I wait the mustering out!

THE PICTURE.

A CALM, sweet face, with earnest eyes
   And thoughtful brow, full-arched above it,
A mouth whose graveness won surprise,
   Whose tender sweetness made one love it;
A face that told how souls aspire
   That look beyond to-day's revealing;
A boy, with all of manhood's fire, —
   A man, with all of boyhood's feeling.

They told his life, his honored name,
   His spotless worth, his spirit's beauty,
His few fair years — yet known to fame,
   His sacrifice for right and duty:
His earnest love, his winning grace, —
   But while they spoke of death and glory,
I only read the silent face,
   And dreamed its eyes told all the story.

The soul that waited not for time,
    But sprang at once to perfect flower,
When the first peal of freedom's chime
    Rang out for the appointed hour;
The answering cry, the answering hand,
    Which brooked no weak or base delay,
But, swift for God and native land,
    Flung life and all it loved away;

Yet saw beyond his loss the gain,
    And laid, with step that would not falter,
His blessed gift of love and pain,
    An offering fair, on Freedom's altar:
Wrapped all the future from his sight,
    Thrust back the ties he might not sever,
Then proud, as one who walks in light,
    Gave up himself to God forever!

GOING AND COMING.

FORWARD!
"On to the front!" the order ran,
    "On to the front the foe to meet;"
They shouldered their muskets, boy and man,
    And marched away through the city street.
Banners flying and drum-beat proud,
    Marshaled them on through the noisy way,
But many a heart in the waiting crowd
    Was faint and sick with its fear that day.

Forward!
"On to the front;" 't was a fearful call,
    With Death before to beckon them on;
Who would be first on the field to fall?
    Who would be left when the rest were
        gone?
Was this the last time, full and free,
    To hear the pulse of the city roll,
Before they gasped in their agony
    With the last deep throb of the parting
        soul?

Forward !

On to the front! From peace and life,
   From wife and child with their clinging
   hands,
To the shock and crash of the fearful strife,
   To the unknown grave in the Southern
   lands.
Yet firm as the beat of their martial feet,
   And strong with a freeman's strength of
   soul,
They marched away through the crowded
   street
   With quiver of trumpet drums loud roll,
                              Forward !

   .   .   .   .   .   .

Home !

With silken folds of the banner torn
   In gaps, with the sunlight streaming
   through,
The bayonets gleam from the muskets worn,
   And stain and dust on the army blue ;
Back from the battle-fields far away,
   Their medals of bronze on cheek and
   brow,
. They came through the city streets to-day, —
Our Legion of Honor we call them now.

Home !
When the word went down to that hell of
    war,
    And the fetid walls where the prisoners
        slept,
God ! what a shout rang near and far
And up to the listening heavens swept !
Eyes that were dry mid the groans of death,
    Hearts unawed by the bullet and sword,
Grew dim and soft with the whispered breath,
    And melted in tears at the well-known
        word.

    Home !
Many had reached it long ago,
    Not the place that our hearts had planned,—
The fireside rest that their feet should know,
    Who came to us back from the direful
        land, —
But a sweeter rest — which never shall
    cease —
    Than the deepest depths of our love could
        give,
Where God Himself is the light of Peace,
    And the ransomed soldiers of freedom live.

Home !
Whether on earth or whether in heaven,
Where lips may touch or prayers arise,
Honor and praise to their names be given
Under the sun or above the skies.
Till the jubilant air shall rise and swell
With strong full shouts of the heart's
delight,
Welcome with clangor of cannon and bell
The bronze-brown heroes of field and fight
Home !

THANKSGIVING, 1863.

GOD of the day and night !
Whose presence dwells, serene and lovely still,
Above all waves of human good or ill,
    In darkness as in light !

When summer skies are fair, —
When Peace and Plenty reign above the land,
The weakest soul can feel Thy guiding hand,
    And read Thy mercy there ;

But when the tempest's might
Sullenly bursts above the faded flowers,
And all that smiled upon this earth of ours
    Is dashed from vale and height, —

It needs a stronger trust,
Beyond the wrecks of hope and light to see
A purer life made beautiful by Thee,
    Whose ways are ever just !

We do not weakly fear
Beneath the roughest blast of Winter's breath,
Nor shrink before his icy calm of death
When all is dark and sere ;

We know he holds the Spring ;
Till flinging back its robe of ice and showers
The sunshine laughs on bees and buds and
    flowers,
And bids its wild birds sing.

Yet do our spirits faint,
When, rolling on the blood-stained cloud of
    war,
We catch the shadow of the strife afar,
And smell the battle taint, —

Forgetting, in our pain,
The Lord of Hosts, who strikes from scenes
    like these
The grandest chords of human destinies,
And makes all bright again !

Teach us O Lord ! to see
With the same faith that laughs the clouds to
    scorn,

Past the dark night, and to the coming morn
    Made glad and fresh by Thee!

    So shall our anthem sweet,
Of Praise and Thanks and Love, swell glad on
    high,
And pierce beyond the clouds of soul and sky
    To seek Thy blessèd feet.

HEARTSICK !

"Is it the tramp of men to battle
Breaking across the silent night,
The stinging roll of the muskets' rattle,
The far-off shock of the deadly fight?
Is it the moan of strong men dying,
Coming across the dreary plain?"
"Mother, only the south wind sighing,
And the falling drops of the summer rain."

"Listen again! where the hill lies glooming,
Flinging its shadow across the grass,
Did you not hear the cannon booming,
And clash of steel from the rocky pass?
Now drawing nearer, now retreating,
Are there not cries on the village green?"
"Only the surf on the dark rocks beating,
And the roll of the thunder dropped be-
tween."

Alas and alas ! When the heart is fearing,
Every shadow has life and weight,

Even the wind, to the spirit's hearing,
  Comes like the call of a beck'ning Fate !
You, O child, in your springtime gladness,
  Only the wrath of the tempest see, —
I, with a longing, sick heart sadness,
  What does the south wind say to me ?

That some place where its breath is falling
  He is fighting, — perhaps is slain ;
That some place where its voice is calling
  He is moaning my name in vain ;
Somewhere under its lonely sighing,
  In broken slumber or deadly strife,
In camp or field is the true heart lying
  That calls you " darling " and calls me
    " wife."

You and I, my little one, nesting
  Safe by his hearthstone, far away, —
What shall we do for our soldier's resting, —
  What *can* we do but wait and pray.
Through all the changes life may ring us,
  Waiting and praying with trust and might,
But most of all when the south winds bring
    us
  A message from him, as they do to-night.

THE PICKET.

Slow across the dull Potomac fades the dim
    November light,
And the darkness, like a mantle, folds the tented
    field from sight ;
In the shadowed wood beside me breaks the
    wind with quiv'ring moan,
        Floating, sighing,
        Falling, dying,
     As I keep my watch alone.

Forward, backward, stern and fearless, till the
    moonbeam's silver ray
Breaks in many a gleaming arrow from my bay-
    onet's point away ;
So I pace the picket lonely, while apart from
    mortal sight
        Watch I 'm keeping
        With the sleeping
    Loved ones far away to-night.

On the morrow comes Thanksgiving, when from
  households far and wide
Round the hearths the children gather, — seek
  once more the old fireside ;
Fill once more the vacant places that they left
  so long ago,
    Self-relying,
    Proudly trying
   All life's unknown joy and woe.

On the morrow comes Thanksgiving ! Not as
  long ago it came,
Bright, without a shade of sorrow lingering round
  its good old name ;
War has waved his crimson banner, and beneath
  its blood stains rest
    All his glory,
    Dim and gory,
   Laid on many a lifeless breast.

Wife and child and aged mother wake at morn
  to bend the knee,
And, around the hearthstone glowing, supplicate
  their God for me ;
Near my vacant chair they gather, blending tears
  amid their prayers, —

He will hear them,
And anear them
Will my spirit kneel with theirs.

Nor is darkness all around us ; we can thank
our God for might,
For the strength which He has given still to
struggle for the Right ;
For the soul so grandly beating in the nation's
onward way,
For the spirit
We inherit
On this new Thanksgiving day !

Still the blue Potomac ripples like a silver
thread below,
And amid the sullen darkness rises high the
camp-fire's glow ;
So I pace the picket lonely, while apart from
mortal sight
Watch I 'm keeping
With the sleeping
Loved ones far away to-night.

VICTORY!

FLASH the news, exultant wire,
  Send it throbbing through the land!
Blaze it like an altar-fire,
  Consecrating heart and hand;
Ring it over streets and lanes,
  Fling it full on land and sea,
Shout on all our hills and plains,
                    Victory!

Dearly bought? Nay, never fear!
  Right is right, whate'er it cost;
He who sees both blood and tear
  Will not count His heroes lost.
What is life when honor dies, —
  What is death when souls are free, —
Which is writ in Heaven's eyes
                    Victory?

If perchance some note of pain,
  Sad as sorrow, sweet and low,
Falls like fall of weeping rain,
  For vanished friend and vanished foe, —

Though your hopes lie cold and pale,
　God's great heart can hear and see,
High above that broken wail,
　　　Victory !

Then flash on exultant wires,
　Send it thrilling through the land !
Blaze it high as altar-fires,
　Consecrating heart and hand ;
God is near us in the strife,
　And whate'er the end may be,
He can make or death or life
　　　Victory !

WOUNDED.

Wounded! my boy? No, it must be another, —
  Left in his gore on that field of the South, —
Gone but ten days from the arms of his
    mother,
  The breath of his kisses yet sweet on my
    mouth.

Wounded! — his head on the battle-field lying,
  Lips gasping out in a feverish moan,
Wounded? — away! why not tell me he's dying,
  Dead ere I reach him, my darling, my son.

Blood gushing out where the sabre stroke cleft
    him,   •
  Blood clotted thick on his hair's sunny light;
Curse on the dastardly hand that has left him,
  Calling my name in his anguish to-night!

I can remember his eager tones falling,
  Kneeling before me, — his head on my
    breast,

"Let me go, mother; our country is calling;
  Give me your blessing, — trust God for the
    rest."

I can remember when drums loudly beating
  Led from the city the troops to their place,
That over all tumult of parting and greeting,
  I heard but one voice, and I saw but one
    face, —

Saw but one face shining calmly and proudly,
  Keeping quick time with the tramp of the
    feet;
Heard but one voice shouting clearly and
    loudly,
  "Good-by, my mother, — trust God till we
    meet."

Now! — O my God! — let my trust be un-
    shaken,
  Lead me beyond the dark shadows to rest;
Wounded, they tell me, but O not forsaken;
  Bring him once more to his place on my
    breast!

THE KEARSARGE.

WE welcome back the war-worn feet
  That trod the Southern plain;
Have we no sign of praise to greet
  Their brothers of the main?
No heart-warm word, no earnest way,
  To show the thought that thrills
When the old Kearsarge rests to-day
  Beneath New England's hills?

Yes! by our faith in manly deeds
  Done thus in noble guise,
The hands that fill our nation's needs
  Are sacred to our eyes:
The hands that raised our Nation's stars
  Above the solemn sea,
And held them, spite of wounds and scars,
  Unconquered, stainless, free!

O moment bright with honest light,
  And rich with honest grace,
When thus the New World held her right
  Before the Old World's face;

Well might the startled echoes wake
    The British lion's trance,
And on their silken standards shake
    The fleur-de-lis of France.

We are too late to catch the first
    Swift glory as it came,
While yet the notes of triumph burst
    From out the lips of Fame:
But not too late to leave our meed
    Of honor's fadeless flowers,
And hail with welcome and God-speed
    These sailor-boys of ours.

O stalwarth arms and loyal hearts
    A Nation holds your name!
The seasons wane, the year departs,
    There is no death for Fame!
Her hands will hold the scroll sublime
    While Freedom's self shall last,
Undimmed, untouched, by change or time,
    Immortal as our past!

WAITING FOR THE NEWS.

HARK! how the mad bells, peal on peal,
   Swell to the jubilant sky,
Ringing a victory's woe and weal
   Out to the passers-by:
Weal for the triumph of right again,
   Woe for the brave lives flown,
And the hearts all dumb with their crushing
    pain,
   That sit with the night alone.

Weal or woe, — which is it for me?
   What have I won from Fame?
How can I tell till I hear and see
   The place they will give his name?
Here I sit like a blinded Fate,
   Waiting what time may bring, —
When I open and enter the Future's gate,
   Shall I meet corpse or king?

What shall I meet? 'T is hard to hope,
   But hardest of all to fear,

When will the mystical future ope
And read me my riddle clear?
Proud with the pride of a soldier's life, —
Stretched on a soldier's bier, —
How has *he* passed the fearful strife?
When will the news be here?

Help me, O God, to know Thee just;
Fold me within Thy love,
Teach me to hold both faith and trust,
Guide me to look above;
Grant me the strength to stand or bow,
As Thy dear will may choose;
Keep me, O Lord, beside Thee now,
While waiting for the news.

IN FAITH AND TRUST.

WHEN May-time fills the charmèd air,
  Across the trees her sweet blooms flinging,
When May-time suns are shining fair,
  And all the woods with song are ringing, —
We bare our Mother Nature's breast
  As first she wakes from winter's sleeping,
And lay the seedlings there to rest,
  In faith and trust for future reaping.

We may not see if bane or blight
  The summer holds, our fond dreams chiding;
We may not read with prophet sight
  What change the far-off days are hiding;
Though storms arise and tempests blow,
  Though Fate its darksome web be folding,
We walk our way, content to know
  That His dear hands our trusts are holding.

Now, too, where battle thunders roar,
  And battle hail of shot is crashing,
On Southern plain and Southern shore
  The lightning of its death-fire flashing;

Where blood-stains dim the glowing sod,
Where pulsing streams of life are flowing,
Where dying eyes are raised to God, —
We plant again fair seed for sowing.

Each brave heart lying still and cold,
    Far, far away from those who love it;
Each grave the quiet hills enfold
    Where some dear face may bend above it;
Each torture-pang of brain and soul,
    Each tear from eyes unused to weeping, —
Within His hands we place the whole,
    And wait in faith the time of reaping.

In Faith and Trust, O God of might!
    No dark despair, no vain repining;
Beyond the depths of sorrow's night
    We see far off the morning shining;
Give us Thy strength, O Wise and Just,
    To wait till Time shall ope the portal,
And perfect faith and perfect trust
    Shall reap their fruit in joy immortal!

OF CHILDHOOD.

AN ANSWER!

'WHAT is the Baby made for?" Why,
  For hugging and kissing, and cooing and
    pressing;
For joy to the heart, and for light to the eye;
  For tossing and tumbling and loving caressing;
    For crowing and crooning and smiling;
    For dimpling and pretty beguiling;
      For fretting,
      And petting,
    And sudden sweet antic, —
      For crying
      And trying
    To make us all frantic;
For trouble and care that can never be paid for,
Perhaps *this* may be what the Baby is made for!

"What is the Baby made for?" Well,
  For ruling the house with a sceptre imperious;
For making, as if by a fairy spell,
  Our working time gay, and our playing time
    serious;

For upsetting waking and sleeping ;
For mixing up smiling with weeping ;
And yet with such total surrender
Of our hearts to his whims and his splendor,
That we kiss the small rod while it schools us,
And love the wee tyrant who rules us :
Helpless and weak, to be cherished and prayed
    for, —
Perhaps *this* may be what the Baby is made for !

"What is the Baby made for ? "   Dear,
    Sometimes I think as a lesson solely
To us who are helpless as Baby here,
    And worthless and poor, that God loves us
        wholly.
        See ! we have naught to commend us
        Save what His mercy doth lend us ;
        Powerless, weak, and forsaken,
    Until His love doth awaken !
        Safely His arms do enfold us,
        Like unto babes He doth hold us ;
        Sheltered, beloved, and protected,
        Pleasantly led and directed, —
        To show that our feeble endeavor
        Is helped by His goodness forever,
With tenderness deeper than ever we prayed for,
Perhaps *this* may be what the Baby is made for !

SLEEPING.

THE violet eyes lie shaded deep
   Beneath the white lids closing ;
The cheeks flushed faint with rosy sleep,
   The dimpled hands reposing ;
The sweet red lips held half apart,
   Smiles coming and retreating ;
God bless and keep the little heart
   Within the white breast beating,
          As baby sleeps.

The tiny, restless, busy feet
   Lie still in cradle nesting ;
The clinging arms fall white and sweet
   Upon the pillow resting ;
Close out the burst of noise and glare,
   Harsh sound, and harsher seeming,
And let the soft, sweet summer air
   Float gently through his dreaming,
          As baby sleeps.

And life and time go hurrying on,
   Their varied meshes weaving ;

And heaven is lost, and heaven is won,
  And joy gives place to grieving ;
The summer comes, the summer flies,
  And brings the autumn's glory, —
While still my darling's violet eyes
  Repeat the same old story, —
      That baby sleeps.

I sit and muse, while yet apace
  The future years are winging,
And think what gifts of love and grace
  Their hidden hands are bringing ;
What paths the little feet may tread,
  What work the hands be moulding,
What crown awaits my darling's head,
  When heart and soul unfolding,
      No longer sleep.

Ah ! hope has many a fairy theme
  That her sweet lips are breathing,
And life has many a golden dream
  That some fond heart is wreathing ; —
But none so glad as those that rise
  In light and beauty blending,
To shine before a mother's eyes,
  Above the cradle bending
      While baby sleeps.

O God of love! whose mercies shine,
  Though all earth's ties may sever,
And thou, whose Motherhood Divine
  Has made thee ours forever,
Guard, guide, and bless, till years have gone,
  And strong with strength supernal,
A conqueror with his glory won,
  He enters life eternal, —
            And baby wakes.

10

LOVE'S DICTIONARY.

WHAT is the sweetest?
The Baby's mouth,
With its pure, soft breathing coming and
going,
Like perfume of winds from the sunny South,
Over the orange and lime-trees blowing.
Dimples hid in the curving tips,
Rose-leaf bloom on the gracious lips,
Tremulous smiling,
Soul beguiling,
This is the sweetest.

What is the brightest?
The Baby's eyes,
A heaven of gladness within them sleeping;
Questioning light that comes and flies,
Moving our hearts to smiles and weeping,
Trust and hope and divinest love,
Caught from the altar-fires above,
Gleaming and glowing,
Joy bestowing,
This is the brightest.

What is the strongest?
>> The Baby's hand,
With its tiny fingers groping and clasping,
Measuring out life's golden sands,
> And strong men's souls in its strange might
>> grasping.
> O what is power and pomp and place
> To the tender touch of its dimpled grace!
>> Clinging, caressing,
>> Leading and blessing,
>> This is the strongest.

MY WEE LOVER.

TELL me what wee lover this is
With his sweet mouth full of kisses ;
With his great eyes, dark and tender,
Full of love's divinest splendor ;
With the lips in bird-like cooing,
Breathing all sweet notes of wooing ;
While the rose-leaf fingers pressing
Win my heart with fond caressing.

Curving grace of red lips smiling,
Sweet eyes bent in love's beguiling,
With the sunlight's golden meshes,
Snared within his deep brown tresses, —
Peach-bloom cheek to my cheek clinging,
Arms to meet my own upspringing,
Heart of gold that all divine is,
Such this wee fond love of mine is.

Kiss and kiss again, my darling !
Care without the gate is snarling,

Angry that we thus can flout him,
Laugh and smile and live without him ;
We have found a better preacher :
Love is still the wisest teacher,
When his lore I thus discover,
Holding fast my wee sweet lover.

MY LITTLE MAN.

My little man is merry and wise,
  Gay as a cricket and blithe as a bird;
Often he laughs and seldom he cries,
  Chatters and coos at my lightest word:
    Peeping and creeping and opening the
      door,
    Clattering, pattering over the floor,
    In and out, round about, fast as he can, —
    So goes the daytime with my little man.

My little man is brimful of fun,
  Always in mischief and sometimes in grief;
Thimble and scissors he hides one by one,
  Till nothing is left but to catch the thief:
    Sunny hair, golden fair, over his brow;
    Eyes so deep, lost in sleep, look at him
      now;
    Baby feet, dimpled sweet, tired as they ran,
    So goes the night-time with my little man.

My little man with cherry-ripe face,
  Pouting red lips and dimpled chin,

Fashioned in babyhood's exquisite grace,
  Beauty without and beauty within, —
    Full of light, golden bright, life as it
      seems,
    Not a tear, not a fear, knows in thy
      dreams ;
    Kisses and blisses now make up its span,
    Could it be always so, my little man ?

My little man the years fly away,
  Chances and changes may come to us all, —
I 'll look for the babe at my side some day,
  And find him above me, six feet tall ;
    Flowing beard hiding the dimples I love,
    Grizzled locks shading the clear brow
      above,
    Youth's promise ripened on Nature's broad
      plan,
    And nothing more left me of my little man.

My little man, — when time shall bow,
  With its hoary weight, my head and thine, —
Will you love me then as you love me now,
  With sweet eyes looking so fond in mine ?
    However strangely my lot may be cast,
    My hope in life's future, my joy in life's
      past,

Loyal and true as your loving heart can,
Say, will you always be my little man?

My little man! perchance the bloom
Of the hidden years, as they come and pass,
May leave me alone, with a wee, wee tomb
Hidden away in the tangled grass.
Still as on earth, so in heaven above,
Near to me, dear to me, claiming my love,
Safe in God's sunshine, and filling his
plan,
Still be *forever* my own little man.

TO EDITH.

Darling little birthday maiden,
  Flower of autumn time,
With what dainty wishes laden
  Shall I weave my rhyme ;
What of all the world has on it
  Seems most fair and dear
To gift the eyes that look upon it
  Wise with one short year ?

Little one, life opens kindly,
  Full of light and fair,
Though you take it all so blindly,
  Sitting smiling there ;
Not a mesh that love could sever
  Tangled round thy feet, —
Could we keep it so forever, —
  Hazel eyes, my sweet !

Who can tell how many changes
  Wait beside the way,
As life's onward pathway ranges
  Farther day by day ;

Yet whatever time may measure
   Has its part to teach,
When the soul, through pain and pleasure,
   Gathers wealth from each.

So, though all a mother's longing
   Waits with passion fond,
With a thousand wishes thronging
   The dim years beyond,
Still I think from all God's giving
   Naught more blest could fall
Than the golden gift of living,
   Gathering strength from all.

Ah ! you scarce see where I 'm drifting,
   Filled with vague surprise,
To my face that pure brow lifting,
   And those hazel eyes !
Do not seek to know, my treasure, —
   Wait, in peace divine ;
All too soon life's pain and pleasure
   Reach us, baby mine

Could I read the years before thee !
   Would I if I could ?
Knowing still God 'watches o'er thee,
   And that He is good.

Rather let me clasp thee, holding
 All the years at bay,
In my life thy life enfolding
 As I do to-day.

So my little birthday maiden,
 Flower of autumn time,
With the heart's best wishes laden
 Take the halting rhyme.
All the gifts in Time's full coffers
 Piled before thy feet,
Show not half the love it offers, —
 Hazel eyes, my sweet.

ROBBIE'S ANGEL!

In the shower and shine of April
  We laid beneath the sod
Our darling, our wee white maiden,
  To bloom in the fields of God;
And the children, who missed her sorely,
  Would talk to me day by day
Of the dear little angel sister,
  Who had wandered so far away!

And they learned to send a greeting,
  Each night as they knelt in prayer,
And thought God told our darling,
  Who listened and heard it there :
For we dared not cloud their gladness,
  Nor speak of our circle riven, —
But as if the chain had lengthened,
  And reached from earth to heaven.
  .   .   .   .   .

When winter snows were whitest,
  And piled into drift on drift,
Another wee nestling reached us, —
  A wonderful Christmas gift !

And the children gathered around it
In beautiful glad surprise
At the size of the baby's fingers, —
The blue of the baby's eyes.

Then Robbie, in eager wonder,
With his dimpled face alight,
Said, " What were you called, you darling,
When you came to our house last night ? "
And when nurse replied, " An angel,"
His great brown eyes grew wide, —
" Oh ! what was your name, sweet angel,
In the house from which you died ? "

AT A BAPTISM.

Dark-eyed baby Natalie, —
With all pure things in accord, —
On this Sabbath of the Lord,
Unto Him we offer thee!
Rich in all thy baby charms,
In His temple to His arms
Do we bring thee, asking there
Fuller meed of faith and prayer,
Safer guidance, richer grace,
Than our mortal hands may trace.

Had we lived in other climes,
Fairer scenes and older times,
Long ago when Fairy Queens
Mingled in our earthly scenes, —
On this day what gifts most sweet
Would be piled before thy feet!
Dower of love, and length of days,
Fadeless beauty, winning ways,
Philters rich in magic art
Conquering for thee every heart,

Or some charm of power untold
Changing all thy words to gold.

Bonny baby Natalie!
Fairies still are left for thee,
In the arts of love more strong
Than the elves of tale and song;
All too poor to them do seem
Earthly gift and earthly dream;
All too short earth's transient hope,
For the soul's immortal scope;
So to-day their hearts have flown
On strong wings to God's white throne,
And in guerdon full and free,
Opened heaven itself to thee,
Dark-eyed baby Natalie.

LILIES AND ROSES.

WHEN a child breathes a pure and earnest
  prayer,
Or cheers with gentle words another's gloom,
In heavenly gardens springs a lily fair,
  Before the angels evermore to bloom.

But when he works with strong and earnest
  will
  Some kindly act, — beneath God's watchful
  eyes
A fragrant rose, more rare and precious still,
  Makes glad the shining fields of Paradise.

So live, dear boy, that each new day may see
Lilies and roses owe their life to thee!

IN SORROW.

MY GRIEFS !

I HAVE a grief against the radiant day,
      In that it fails to shine
      On those dear eyes of mine
That used to greet its coming. Day by day
They lie, close shut in shadows cold and gray.

I have a grief against the silent night,
      In that it fails to rest
      Close folded on its breast
The little feet I love, whose echo light
Made all the dreams that filled my future bright.

I have a grief against the smiling earth,
      Because within its round
      My little hearts have found
But wee, wee-graves; while I, who gave them
      birth,
Stand lonely, weeping by my darkened hearth.

    .   .   .   .   .   .

" O torn spirit ! Tried and troubled soul,"
    Methought a voice replied,
    " God's heaven is fair and wide,
With one swift bound, for earth's poor meagre
    dole,
Thy little hearts have won and grasped the
    whole.

" Fair on the shining hills of Paradise
    The wee feet rest and play
    In light and love alway ;
And God's great glory lights the wakened eyes
Beyond the shadows of our clouded skies.

" Look up ! Look up ! His ways are ever kind,
    His leadings not in vain ;
    Thine is not loss, but gain ;
Life, Love, and Joy, thy new-born angels
    find, —
All heaven rejoices ! Thou alone art blind ! "

"LORD, KEEP OUR MEMORY GREEN!"

WHEN, in the first wild throes of grief,
The sick heart turns from all relief,
And backward counting, sad and slow,
An hour, a week, a month ago
To days ere yet the light had flown
From those dear eyes we called our own, —
We ask of God the seal to set :
"How long, O Lord, ere we forget?"

For still to live through unknown years,
Lost voices ringing in our ears, —
Lost faces held in memory's grasp, —
Lost hands that never more we clasp, —
And feet whose steps have died away
Walking beside us day by day, —
Seems all too hard for love's regret,
And so we pray, " Let us forget !"

But when above life's troubled springs
We feel the stir of angels' wings,

And His dear blessing, sweet and slow,
Drops on the wounded hearts below ;
When Faith ascends the golden stair,
Of love and hope and trust and prayer, —
Though grief and pain may linger yet
We would not, if we could, forget !

No ! Not one motion full of grace,
Nor change of the beloved face,
Nor pouting of the baby lips,
Nor touch of tiny finger tips,
Nor cooing pat of rosy palms,
Nor sudden griefs and sudden calms,
Nor roguish smile, nor dainty fret,
Would we, for all the world, forget.

" Lord, Keep our Memory green !" — May each
Sweet babbling flow of baby speech,
Each trick of eye and hand and voice,
Still make our brooding thought rejoice :
The lips, the cheek, the forehead fair,
The dimpling smile, the floating hair, —
Still in our hearts let these be set,
Nor let us, evermore, forget !

DEAD !

DEAD ! That is the word
That rings through my brain till it crazes !
    Dead, while the Mayflowers bud and blow,
    While the green creeps over the white of
        the snow,
While the wild woods ring with the song of the
        bird,
    And the fields are a-bloom with daisies !
        ˈ

    See ! Even the clod
Thrills, with life's glad passion shaken ;
    The vagabond weeds with their vagrant
        train
    Laugh in the sun and nod in the rain,
The blue sky smiles like the eye of God, —
    Only my dead do not waken !

    Dead ! — There is the word
That I sit in the darkness and ponder !
    Why should the river, the sky, and the sea
    Babble of summer and joy to me,

While a strong true heart with its pulse un-
   stirred
Lies hushed in the silence yonder?

Lord! Lord! How long
Ere we rise to Thy heights supernal
   Ere the soul may read what Thy spirit
   saith;
" Life that must fade, is not life but death.
Lift up thine eyes O soul! Be strong ;
   For Death is the Life Eternal! "

GOD'S ACRE.

WHERE God's fair acre rests enthroned
  Above the sloping meadow,
I sit beside the wee, wee mound
  That holds my heart in shadow.

Around me rose and lily bloom,
  Above the wild bird passes,
And violets faint with love's perfume
  Lie hid in tall, green grasses.

The city's clustered steeples gleam,
  Near thought of heaven bestowing,
As if in some fair pictured dream,
  Across the landscape showing.

All thought of life and life's unrest
  Are hushed within this portal,
The peace that fills each quiet breast
  Breathes only love immortal.

And yet — and yet — my heavy eyes
  Can scarcely see for weeping,

The tender, radiant summer skies,
In calm, blue silence sweeping.

O birds that sing! O flowers that wave!
In vain your joys are given, —
The shadow of one little grave
Can reach from earth to heaven.

THE ANSWERED PRAYER.

I KNEW a pair of brave, brown eyes,
  So rich in life, so bright in glee,
That naught beneath God's radiant skies
  Was dearer than their light to me :
    Full of love and winning wild,
    Blithe and gay and undefiled,
  "Lord !" we prayed, "so keep our child !'

I knew a pair of large, dark eyes
  Soft smiling in·a little face,
So sweetly sad, so gravely wise,
  So full of childhood's pensive grace
    As they drooped beneath our kiss :
  "God !" we asked, "O grant him this,
  Joy and peace and purest bliss !"

I knew a pair of clear blue eyes
  So lately from the angels riven,
The light they brought from Paradise
  Still lent a gleam to earth of heaven :

"Father!" cried we, "keep afar
Through life's battle stain and scar,
Grief to cloud, or sin to mar."

.   .   .   .   .   .

This did we ask, as day's fair dawn
  Crept smiling from the night's dark breast,
And this, when shadowy eve had drawn
  Its darkling vail across the west:
    He to whom the prayer had flown
    Answered, bending from His throne,
    Not in our way, but His own!

    Brave, brown eyes will never know
    Shade of sin, or tear of woe;
    Soft, dark eyes will gladly shine,
    Full of light of love divine;
    Sweet, blue eyes with angel smile
    Hail the heaven they left awhile.

For sweeping through the silence dim,
  The while we stood with reverent breath,
God's angels took them up to Him,
  Beyond the gates of sin and death!
    God, who holds our darlings there,
    Teach our weak, weak hearts to bear
    This, Thy answer to our prayer!

OUR ANGEL.

SEVENTEEN months our wee white maid
  Grew in the sunshine fair and sweet,
Till the dearest music of life was played
  By the touch of her hands and the fall of
      her feet;
Then as the dawn of the·April day
  Wooed new life to the winter sod,
Our little white maiden turned away,
  And went to dwell in the smile of God.

Ah well.! we know the fairest years
  Of the brightest future ever we planned
Are dark with sorrow and pain and tears
  Compared with the joy of that blissful land.
But O for the woe of the empty hands,
  And the longing heart, and the tear-dimmed
      eyes,
Trying to reach where our darling stands,   ·
  And follow her footsteps in Paradise.

Little white angel up in heaven
  Safe in His arms whose smile is Love,

Does the wailing cry of our fond hearts riven
  Ring through the peace of the courts above?
Does the shadow of grief, like a vague surprise,
  Reach through the glory around the throne,
Drawing thy grave, sweet, earnest eyes
  Down through the worlds to meet our own?

You cannot answer back, my Sweet,
  But One who came down to us long ago
Gathered the children about His feet,
  And taught us the lesson we fain would
    know, —
That if but a glimpse of the light above
  Could flash for a moment on earth's dull
    pain,
We 'd lose all else that is ours to love,
  Rather than beckon thee back again.

'T is not forever we say farewell, —
  Child of our heart, so pure, so fair!
We will kiss the lips we have loved so well,
  And play with the rings of the soft brown
    hair;
For I know when my soul in the silence waits
  The wonderful kingdom of God to see,
Down like a star through the beautiful gates
  My little white angel will come to me.

TWO BIRTHDAYS.

ONE little year ago to-day,
  My darling's birthday face above,
I wished the world's best gifts away
    To crown my love.

How could I dream of grief so near,
  How could I shrink from coming harms,
When thus I held her, fond and dear,
    Within my arms?

When shining from the smiling eyes,
  And laughing round the baby lips,
I saw the future years arise
    Without eclipse.

Folding her closer to my breast, —
  Of all the hopes that love would crave
How could I dream that naught would rest
    But this small grave?

.   .   .   .   .   .

O saddened heart, bowed sorely down
  Beneath the harsh weight of thy loss,

Better that hers should be the crown
And thine the cross.

This light across the darkness drifts :
More than we asked our God has given ;
We only prayed for earth's poor gifts, —
He gave her heaven !

ALL-SAINTS.

O BLESSED ones who rest at last
    Above all sense of grief and loss,
Who mounted through the thorny past
    To find the crown above the cross, —

Forgotten now the prison bars,
    The fire, the steel, the martyr pain,
The balm of love has healed the scars,
    And only joy and peace remain.

To-day we wreathe no single shrine,
    We call no holy name apart,
But turn to all whom Love divine
    Has gathered up to His great heart.

Teach us, O spirits glorified,
    To climb the heights your feet have trod!
Be still our help whate'er betide,
    All-Saints, to lead all souls to God.

A DEAD SUMMER.

WHAT lacks the summer?
Not roses blowing,
Nor tall white lilies with fragrance rife,
Nor green things gay with the bliss of growing,
Nor glad things drunk with the wine of life,
Nor flushing of clouds in blue skies shining,
Nor soft wind murmurs to rise and fall,
Nor birds for singing, nor vines for twining, —
Three little buds I miss, no more,
That blossomed last year at my garden
door, —
And that is all.

What lacks the summer?
Not waves a-quiver
With arrows of light from the hand of dawn,
Nor drooping of boughs by the dimpling river,
Nor nodding of grass on the windy lawn,
Nor tides upswept upon silver beaches,
Nor rustle of leaves on tree-tops tall,
Nor dapple of shade in woodland reaches, —

Life pulses gladly on vale and hill,
But three little hearts that I love are still, —
    And that is all.

What lacks the summer ?
           O light and savor,
And message of healing the world above !
Gone is the old-time strength and flavor,
  Gone is its old-time peace and love !
Gone is the bloom of the shimmering mead-
    ows,
  Music of birds as they sweep and fall, —
All the great world is dim with shadow,
    Because no longer mine eyes can see
    The eyes that made summer and life for
    me, —
        And that is all.
    12

FOR SPECIAL OCCASIONS.

THE LAST BULLETIN.

GARFIELD, SEPTEMBER, 1881.

DAY after day as morning skies did flame, —
"How fares our Liege?" we cried with eager
    breath, —
"How fares our Liege, who fights the fight
    with death?"
And ever with fresh hope the answer came.

Until that solemn midnight when the clang
Of woful bells tolled out their tale of dread,
That he, the good and gifted one, was dead,
And through his weeping land the message
    rang !

Then in the darkness every heart was bowed :
While thinking on the direful ways of Fate,
Where Love could thus be overthrown by
    Hate, —
"So wrong hath conquered right !" we said
    aloud :

.

"If this be life, what matter how it flies;
 What strength or power or glory crowns a
   name ;
 What noble meed of honesty or fame,
Since all these gifts were his, — and there he
   lies

Blighted by malice! Woe's the day! and dead
 While yet the fields of his most golden prime
 Are rich in all the pomp of summer time,
With all their ripening wealth unharvested! "
 .   .   .   .

Thus fares it with our Liege? Nay, doubting
   soul,
 Not thus ; but grandly raised to nobler
   height
 Of strength and power and most divine delight, —
At one swift breath made beautiful and whole !

Nor mocked by broken hope or shattered
   plan,
 By some pale ghost of duty left undone,
 By haunting moments wasted one by one,
But crowned with that which best becometh
   man.

Holding with brimming hands his heart's de·
    sire ;
While the fierce light of these last glorious
    days,
Blazing on each white line of thought and
    ways,
Touches his record with immortal fire !

THE BIRTHNIGHT.

MOORE CENTENNIAL.

STRIKE a jubilant chord, O Earth, for the birth
of the poet!
Welcome his conquering feet with harmony
vibrant and strong ;
Arch of the smiling sky, and blue sea ripple
below it,
Welcome his conquering feet, who comes in
the glory of song.

Flush of the incoming day and glowing of sunset splendor,
Silent feet of the night treading her shining
ways,
Crooning of summer winds in lullaby dreamy
and tender,
Welcome the birth of the poet with pæans
of triumph and praise.

For he is the breath of thy soul, the pulse of
    the heart of thy being,
He is the voice of thy voice which speaks
    from the leaf and sod,
Falling in healing and balm on spirit and eyes
    unseeing,
And changing their darkness to light, like
    touch of the chrism of God.

O windswept harp of Innisfail
    Wake from thy sleep to-night,
Not faint with sorrow's lingering wail,
    But glad with life's delight!
For he who gave thy notes to fame
    And love and joy of yore,
Brings the fair glory of his name
    To wreathe thy strings once more.

His glory! Aye! The statesman's hand
    May fail with failing breath,
The thought which nerved the Patriot's brand
    Go down with him to death;
But he whose song divine can thrill
    A nation's depths, shall last

Through every phase of doubt or ill,
  Immortal as her past.

Thou soul of love! Thou heart of fire!
  That flamed for Erin's sake ;
Whose light bade each fond hope aspire,
  Whose warmth kept life awake, —
If, at thy name, the thought which starts
  Finds voice in faltering phrase,
'T is that we hold thee in our hearts
  Too deep for idle praise.

But while across Avoca's vale
  The shades of fancy rest,
While the last roses fade and pale
  Above the summer's breast, —
While valor lives, or young love thrills
  The changeful moods of men,
The charm which all thy music fills
  Shall live and breathe again !

And we, who of the whole broad earth
  Can never quite forget
That race and creed and common birth
  Have brought thee nearer yet, —

Thus hail thee whom their souls have known,
Thus hold thy memory shrined,
Thy spirit for thy land alone,
Thy fame for all mankind!

IN MEMORIAM.

(MRS. EDWIN BOOTH.   FEBRUARY 20, 1863.)

Kiss her good-night!
Then let the waiting angel take her hand
To lead her feet across the shining strand
Where life, serene and beautiful, awaits
The coming guest before the golden gates!
Kiss her good-night!

Close the dear eyes
That never more shall fill with unshed tears,
Or dim before the fading touch of years,
But bright with light eternal, from above
Shall guide the treasures of her earthly love.

Smooth the soft hair,
And fold above the silence of the breast
Palm touching palm, her quiet hands to rest,
Fair hands that through all change of good or
ill
Still wove the sunshine of her Master's will.

Wreathe the white brow
In blossoms pure and sweet as her young life,
Which crowned the names of maiden and of
    wife
With all of loveliness that God hath given
To win the trust of earth, the crown of heaven.

Then lead *him* here !
The husband of her soul, whose swift feet came
With eager heart on fire and eyes aflame,
Yet all too late to catch the failing breath,
Or touch her lips before the kiss of death.

Kiss her good-night ; —
She sleeps to wake beneath those fairer skies
Whose light shall chase the shadows from her
    eyes ;
Where, soon or late, all passing terror scorning
Her lips will greet us with a glad "Good
    Morning ! "
Kiss her good-night !

A WEDDING–DAY.

JUNE, 187–.

GLAD with the perfect light of sea and sky,
  And sweet June blossoms trembling on their
    stalks,
  And roses tangled near fair garden walks,
And tuneful wild birds, singing as they fly, —
Glad too with each fair promised hope that
    dwells
  Within the fruitful bosom of the year,
  So dawns the golden day on which we hear
The happy music of thy wedding bells !
O friend, whose steps so lightly turn aside
  To enter on the new and chosen way,
  May each glad type that Heaven hath strewn
    to-day
Of joy and love before the white-robed bride
  Bloom in the fuller sunshine of thy life,
  And crown with bliss the future of the wife.

RESURRECTION!

LINCOLN.   EASTER, 1865.

ONCE more across the Winter's gloom
  The Springtime calls with balmy breath,
  Shakes all the trancèd calm of death,
And bids it wake to sudden bloom ;

Flashes across the upland slope
  And on the mountain-tops unfurled
  Flings out her standards to the world, —
Fit emblem of our future hope ;

Woos with a long sweet summer note
  From where the Southern sunshine smiles,
  The minstrels of our forest aisles,
To fill the wood with tuneful throat, —

And, resting on the barren plain,
  Lifts her fair hands in blessing fond,
  And on the waiting land beyond
Writes " Resurrexit " once again.

To-day, a cloud is in the air;
    A vail across the sunshine drifts
    Whose sombre shadow scarcely lifts
To show the promise hiding there.

A nation's sorrow, still and deep
    And darkly wrapped in shroud and pall,
    Brings mourning to the hearts of all,
And tears from eyes unused to weep.

What blame, if for a little space
    We cannot pierce the gathered gloom,
    Nor look beyond the open tomb,
But only watch the pale, dead face;

What blame, if shrinking from the blow,
    The pleasant paths of life should seem
    But some false fading fleeting dream, —
And change be writ on all below.

———

But not for long; the dread shall cease
    And laugh our broken faith to scorn,
    For us in some fair dawning morn,
For him in God's eternal peace.

For us in that deep strength that springs
   From some swift blow divinely deep,
   That wakes the slumbering soul from sleep
And lifts it to sublimer things. _

For both — the grave mark rolled away
   The stain of blood, the shock of war
   Lost in the light of peace afar,
The Springtime's Resurrection Day!

A WORD AT PARTING.

TO. F. P.

PERCHANCE because I saw thee first in June,
  When the soft touches of the amorous breeze,
  Played coyly with the tresses of the trees,
And glad skies flashed in summer's golden
    noon, —

When with all precious messages of love
  The fair earth teemed, the shining seas grew
    bright,
  And star beams pierced the odorous dusky
    night,
Like eyes of angels looking from above, —

Perhaps for this thy memory hath grown
  A perfumed thought, a fair and sunny thing,
  Which each new summer back to life will
    bring,
And keep amid its treasures as its own!

But for thy gracious reverence of thought,
  And grave eyes tender smiling, and the
    sweet
  Serene low voice with kindliness replete,
Which good from evil evermore hath brought, —

For pleasant neighborhood, and friendly face,
  The memory of thy presence still shall be
  A picture full of richer tints to me
Than any limned by summer's passing grace.

And life may be with better things in tune, —
  With happier dreams to make a sad hour
    bright
  With some new pulse of freshness and de-
    light,
Perchance, — because I saw thee first in June.

IN MEMORIAM.

(GEN. P. R. GUINEY.)

LARGE heart and brave ! Tried soul and true !
   How thickly in thy life's short span
All strong sweet virtues throve and grew,
   As friend, as hero, and as man
Unmoved by thought of blame or praise,
   Unbought by gifts of power and pride,
Thy feet still trod Time's devious ways
   With Duty as thy law and guide.

God breaks no mould so nobly rare
   As shrined of old heroic men ;
In lives like thine, as pure as fair,
   Earth's golden knighthood breathes again
Amid a world of sordid greed,
   Of paltry aims, of perjured trust ;
With soul as stainless as thy creed
   We knew thee strong and pure and just.

23

And still shall know, O friend beloved !
   Thy spirit holds no place with death ;
Our eyes are dim, our hearts are moved,
   But thou hast felt His kindly breath.
So short, so swift thy pang of birth
   Ere dawned the heaven you longed to see,
We bear the pain who wait on earth,
   But all the glory fell to thee !

ODE.

CATHOLIC UNION FESTIVAL, NOVEMBER 13, 1873.

I.

SPIRIT of love Divine!
Come from Thy holy place beside the throne;
Bid light Eternal shine,
Make the great glory of Thy presence known!
Touch our pale lips with flame,
Rouse our weak hearts' desire, —
Come as of old God's burning message came,
Crowning His chosen ones with tongues of fire;
Banish the powers of strife,
Banish the shapes of ill,
Lead unto heavenly life
Souls that would work Thy will:
Bid light Eternal shine,
Spirit of love Divine!

II.

God the Father, — Holy One,
God the Son, whose brow doth rest
On the Virgin Mother's breast,
God the Spirit, — Three in One!

Send the blessed sisters three,
Faith and Hope and Charity,
Unto our hearts, where full of joy we stand,
Lifting glad hands in this our glorious land, —
And in one bond of Union, strong and sweet,
    Bearing the fairest gifts our lives have
    known,
To lay them humbly at the sacred feet
    Of him who sits upon Thine earthly throne.

III.

Lo ! where he sits beneath Italian skies !
Where from the shadow of his prison bars
His soul flames out and upward, — as the stars
    That burn serene though earthly clouds
    arise !
Man cannot strip the glory from his brow,
Nor can the cruel walls restrain the tide
Of all his children's love and joy and pride,
Surging through sea and land to greet him now ;
        Bright amid the names that shine
        In that grand unbroken line
Reaching back through circling ages to the far
    off shores of time, —
To the days when Christ gave Peter his last
    pledge of love sublime !

IV.

O Great and Good! Benign of heart and face!
Whose hand hath paused amid its many cares,
Sending a white-winged messenger of grace
To answer with its blessing our weak prayers!
Here, from the shores that first Columbus trod
To win a world for mankind and for God,
List to the burst of loud and long acclaim,
Teaching our skies the homage due thy name!
Behold the lifted hand, the lighted brow,
As Priest and Prelate with their people bow,
While the long billows of the Western main
Roll with our greeting back and hail thee once
    again!

V.

    And thou, O Mother of our race!
Above whose brow another star arisen
Crowns thee IMMACULATE through Earth and
    Heaven, —
    Hail, Mary, full of Grace!
Youngest amid the nations, still we claim
To hold most dear thine honor and thy name;
Oh! be at once our solace and our rest,
Of all our guides the truest and the best;

Through every grief that clouds a world like
    this,
Be still our star of heaven, our hope of bliss.

VI.

We look beyond the years,
And lo! the gyves that bind our feet are riven,
The banner of our Faith flung high to heaven
    Amid our prayers and tears ; —
The Cross, meet emblem of our strength and
    pride,
Lifts its fair arms and spreads protection wide,
While dedicated to its glory stand
The wealth, the strength, the promise of our
    land ;
    Above the wrecks of error and of time
    The Rock of Peter rears its height sublime,
        And within its grateful shade
        Peace and virtue undismayed,
Nurtured and sheltered in the sacred sod,
Raise their brave fronts and seek the face of
    God ;
While in one grand accord, from sea to sea,
Faith's hymns of triumph rise from millions
    yet to be !

TO DR. JACOB BIGELOW.

(ON HIS 89TH BIRTHDAY.)

O HEAD that wears the kindly state
　　God grants to favored men !
Slight bowed beneath the reverend weight
　　Of fourscore years and ten ;
O hand that worked with earnest might
　　The thoughtful brow's behest,
And hewed a path for truth and right
　　Where other feet might rest, —

What wish is left for us to frame
　　That hope or pride hath known
Of love or trust or honest fame
　　But life hath made thine own ?
Amid the wreaths our hearts entwine
　　We hide no withered leaves,
Where autumn suns serenely shine
　　Above thy ripened sheaves.

All joy is thine that good life brings
　　To memory true and fond.

For eyes grown dim to earthly things
    See clearer light beyond.
The message as of old it ran
    Still to our hearts is given,
And man who loves his fellow man
    Is still the nearest Heaven.

Hail and Godspeed ! May golden days
    Yet wait thy lingering feet,
Love rest on thy accustomed ways,
    Fond hands be stretched to greet ;
Till, rounding all His poorer gifts
    Earth's varying pathway trod,
The passing shadow falls, — then lifts
    And bears thy soul to God.

L'ENVOI.

(TO R. F.   MAY, 1876.)

O FRIEND and Father! if this parting time
  Held not, within its shadow hid away,
  The dawn of greeting for some fairer day,
We scarce could lend thee to that brighter
      clime, —
We scarce could see thy longing feet depart,
  Nor look so calmly on the well loved face,
  Nor say farewell with such an easy grace
If still we did not hold thee heart to heart.
So thus Godspeed : go tread each varied scene
  That now thy poet fancy loves to paint,
  Kneel at the shrine of hero and of saint, —
Where God yet bends to show His power
      supreme ;
Grow rich in all that Life from Time can
      wrest ;
  Be changed by deeper joys and holier trust;
  But when we hail thee, Priest revered and
      just,
Be still the same in all we love the best !

TO R. F.

MAY, 1880.

THERE be all kinds of parting, — some which
    rend
    The very soul with bitter sense of pain,
And, tearing from us the beloved friend,
    Leave wounds which gape while life and
    thought remain.

And some, which lightly met and lightly passed,
    Like cloudwreaths tossed beneath a summer
    sky,
A moment's shadow on the spirit cast,
    But leave the clear sun shining as they fly.

Yet some there are, more blessed than the
    rest,
    Which know of parting but the name alone,
So deeply in each tried and faithful breast
    The spreading roots of mutual trust have
    grown ;

So fairly, through the swiftly passing years
  Has friendship bloomed, with changing time
    and breath,
With holy thought that strengthens and endears,
  With love that mocks at chance and laughs
    at death.

If in our hearts to-night, — O friend revered
  Above the common lot of common men, —
By each best hope of love and life endeared,
  The sense of loss falls blindly now and then ;

Yet do we feel with every throb of grief
  The straining of some bond, so strong and pure
That the sore spirit works its own relief
  And firmly rises, braver to endure.

There is no parting that can take thee hence ;
  There are no ties that thus so lightly fall ;
Through every pulse of upward life and sense,
  Holding thy heart, we hold thee once for all.

And howsoever chance or fate divide,
  Or lands or sea between our paths be thrown,
Still will we share thy hope, thy joy, thy pride,
  Still will we claim and call thee all our own.

TO ——.

My heart is gone !
It went last night — when twilight gray
Was gathering up the light of day ;
And ever since my pulses flow,
In solemn beatings calm and slow,
And thought goes wandering on and on
Where with my love my heart is gone !

Mine eyes are dark !
They dimmed last night when through the street
I watched far off his parting feet, —
And when their echoing tread was still,
A shadow gathered dark and chill,
And ever since no light I mark,
My heart is gone, — mine eyes are dark !

Mine ears are closed !
Though baby coos upon my knee,
And claps his hands in baby glee,
Though kindly voices murmur near,
And bring me words of love and cheer,

His parting voice my heart will hide
And heed nor hear aught else beside

        Till days have flown,
And some bright morning comes, — and then
Mine ears will hear the voice again,
Mine eyes will shine through happy tears,
My soul will fling aside its fears,
And through the smiling autumn weather,
My heart and love come back together
        When days have flown!

FOR THE GOLDEN JUBILEE OF THE SISTERS OF CHARITY.

MAY 14, 1882.

WHEN at the city's gates
Some great one enters in,
Whose name is writ by the Eternal Fates
Time's honored roll within ;
When from the battle-fields
The conquering hosts return,
Bearing aloft on fair, victorious shields
The laurels brave men earn, —
With cannon-burst and blare of echoing sound
We hail their entering feet,
While the glad clamor of the joyous crowd
Fills all the surging street.

O daughters of the Cross,
Not with such loud acclaim
Your strong, sweet souls, that soothe the pain
of loss,
Have stormed the heights of Fame ;

Not with the clang of bell,
  Nor throbbing beat of drum,
Nor lusty shouts that echoing rise and swell,
  Your conquering legions come;
But softly, with the slow and noiseless tread,
  Of Him who quelleth strife,
Who opes the gate of glory to the dead,
  And bids them enter life.

Yet from your gentle hands
  Life's fiercest phantoms fly:
The battle-field, the plague-infested lands,
  Find hope and mercy nigh!
Even from Sin's drear night
  The veil of darkness lifts,
And stars of heaven, with mild, persuasive
      light,
  Shine through the broken rifts;
While soft as summer winds that breathe and
      blow
  Above the winter's sod,
Your message comes to frozen hearts below,
  And warms them back to God.

For Mercy's work no creed
  Confines your earnest will, —

Wherever misery tells its tale of need,
  There bend your footsteps still;
Pure as the lily's cup,
  Undimmed and undefiled,
Your stainless hands do lift the fallen up,
  And soothe the orphaned child.
Burning with love, and strong with heavenly
      grace,
  You seek the wanderer's side,
Nor Jew nor Gentile see in any face,
  But His — the Crucified !

Ye who have conquered bliss,
  Ye who have won the crown,
What can the empty praise of worlds like this
  Add to your fair renown ?
What can our heart's desire
  Offer of gifts or grace
To you, who burning with the sacred fire,
  Shall look upon His face ?
For, O Beloved of the risen Lord,
  Though Faith may mountains move,
And Hope point onward to the soul's reward,
  None enters in but Love !

www.ingramcontent.com/pod-product-compliance
Lightning Source LLC
Chambersburg PA
CBHW030825270326
41928CB00007B/903